Dear Michael

Just a reminder of the Arthur
"fan" club of King Edwards -
Cricket

Enjoyed my time with you &
James watching cricket &
ferrying to various grounds

Much love to you

Dad G
xxxx

Changing Rooms 2

The Cricket Pavilions
of Hampshire and the Isle of Wight

Robert Elliott

Foreword by Tim Tremlett

To Nick

Robert Elliott

Best wishes

27. April. '17

Published by
George Mann Publications
Easton, Winchester,
Hampshire SO21 1ES
georgemann@gmp.co.uk
01962 779944

A CIP catalogue record for this book
is available from the British Library

ISBN 9781907640209

George Mann Publications

Contents

Acknowledgments

Thanks are due to:

All the club officials who have answered calls or e-mails requesting details of their Club or ground and the writers of Club histories that can be found on the world-wide web.

Chris and Annette Booth (The Froyle Archive). Who supplied the Lower Froyle photograph.

Roger Dean. Who donated the photograph of a painting of the old Chandler's Ford pavilion.

George Mann. Who prepared and produced this book.

Ivor Robbins. For the Preshaw & Holt photograph.

Harvey Saunders. Who edited the text, and for the Norman Court School photographs.

Bob Symonds and Mike Porter. Who accompanied me on some of the journeys.

Tim Tremlett. Who wrote the Foreword.

Mike Vimpany. Who helped with the Southern League history, and the picture of Montefiore.

Nick Wood. For the Wootton photograph.

Eastleigh and District Local History Society. Who gave the photograph of the old Fleming Park pavilion.

English-Heritage. For the photograph of the Osborne House pavilion.

Photographs

Except for the those acknowledged above, and the back cover image of the Fawley pavilion from the 1940s, all the photographs are the author's own work,

Back cover

Fawley. Pretty and cosy, but where did they go when it rained?

Front cover

Rotherwick. A beautiful pavilion in a beautiful location. Just perfect.

Foreword

New, old, big, small, grand, and not so grand, your favourite cricket pavilion will forever remind you of famous victories against all the odds, or swashbuckling heroics followed by hysterical celebrations grossly exaggerated by a fading memory.

Images of splintered floorboards, faulty electrics, and a leaking roof remind you of times spent huddled in a cramped space listening to a Captain's inspirational words, or more likely, sheltering from the miserable summer weather.

Bob Elliott loves his sport but cricket holds a special place, and this book will capture the imagination of cricketers, scorers, spectators, and umpires who have spent time at one or more of the incredible number of grounds that he has visited across Hampshire and the Isle of Wight. I have no doubt that this book and the atmosphere created through its wonderful pictures will bring a great deal of enjoyment to those who pick it up.

Tim Tremlett

Hampshire Cricket League President and former Hampshire County Cricket Club player

Lost Grounds

Many cricket grounds are now not used, but these are some that have gone for ever.

CHANDLER'S FORD	Hursley Road	Chandler's Ford CC
HAVANT	IBM Havant Plant	IBM South Hants CC
LYMINGTON	The Ampress Works Ground	Wellworthy CC
MARCHWOOD	Road-Sea Park	Road-Sea CC
PORTSMOUTH	Civil Service Ground, Copnor	A.S.W.E. CC
PORTSMOUTH	The East Hampshire Ground	
SOUTHAMPTON	Antelope Ground	Hampshire CCC
SOUTHAMPTON	Montefiore	Southampton University CC
SOUTHAMPTON	Northlands Road	Hampshire CCC, Deanery CC
SOUTHAMPTON	Moorgreen Cricket Ground	West End CC
WINCHESTER	Olivers Battery	Olivers Battery CC
WINCHESTER	West Hill	West Hill CC

Introduction

This book is about pavilions. Once, many of the pavilions at grass-roots level were just changing rooms. After the game we went to the pub, often unwashed! Kit-bags were not much bigger than hand-bags. The 'coffins' used these days are bigger than the club kit-bag of then. Tea was often taken outside on the grass. Now most have well-equipped kitchens, showers and licensed bars, but some of those old-style pavilions remain.

There is money available for those prepared to work for it. Several organisations give grants to improve facilities at sports grounds and many cricket clubs have taken advantage. Some leagues have sponsors. There are advertising signs around many grounds. Also, increasingly popular are the multi-purpose buildings that are springing up, even in the smallest villages.

Some say that cricket is a dying game. It is true that there is less cricket in schools. However, the recreational game survives, as can be seen here in Hampshire where we boast that our League is perhaps the largest in the world. The clubs have largely taken over what the schools used to do. Many have junior age-group set-ups, with qualified coaches and a lot more unpaid volunteers doing the donkey-work. This allows them to feed the extra teams that have been created for senior cricket. Until the 1970s it was unusual for clubs to have more than one team. In 2016, 114 of the 175 clubs in the Hampshire League had more than one team, twelve of them had four or more. Women's cricket has seen growth as well. Eighteen clubs entered women's teams in the Hampshire League. With all these extra teams in League cricket, the clubs with three or more need an extra pitch to fulfil their fixtures. Some clubs have been able to build second grounds, but the rest have had to find a ground-share arrangement, or use public parks.

There is no need to despair of the future of recreational cricket just yet. After all, it was club cricket that invented the version of the game the professionals market as 20/20, which they seem to see as the future. The limited-over versions are what our

Evening and Saturday Leagues have been playing for years. However, we have seen changes. Friendly matches played to time rather than a fixed amount of overs, have largely died out. All-day games, with lunch and tea, are very rare. League cricket is the norm on Saturday and mid-week, but Friendly Sunday time-cricket still goes on and for some clubs, mainly from the villages, it is the only version of game they play. But, as I said at the start, this is about pavilions . . .

The book is divided into three parts:

1. Southern Premier, and Hampshire League, Grounds.

2. Other Mainland Grounds.

3. Isle of Wight Grounds.

Part 2 includes some pavilions and grounds that no longer exist, and clubs that don't play in the Hampshire League.

Some clubs don't play in leagues of the county they live in and over the years the county boundary has changed, so included are many from Dorset, Wiltshire, Berkshire, Surrey, and West Sussex. Similarly some Hampshire clubs play in competitions in those counties. Hopefully, most have been found, but the Longstock, Buller Barracks, and Osborne House examples were found only after chance remarks, so there will be treasures out there still waiting to be discovered.

Where it has been difficult to find construction or opening details of every pavilion, appropriate historical details of clubs or grounds have been included.

Bob Elliott
January 2017

❖ PART 1 ❖

Southern Premier, and Hampshire League, Grounds

The Southern League started in 1969 with eleven clubs, two of which never competed in the Hampshire League: Bournemouth Amateurs (Dean Park) and South Hants Touring Club (St Helens). They were joined in 1971 by Hyde Ramblers (North Walls) and Southampton University (Montefiore and Wellington Sports Ground). The Hampshire Academy (Rose Bowl Nursery) joined in 2002 and became the fifth team not to have had a team in the Hampshire League. In 2016 the Southern League was made up of forty teams from thirty-four clubs.

The Hampshire League began on Saturday 26 April 1973 with a a match between Hayling Island and Portsmouth & Southsea. There were seventy clubs in two County, and three Regional, divisions. There was also a Supplementary division of eleven clubs, who would join the League in 1974. There were no Second XIs.

In 2016 there were 361 teams from 175 clubs. Of these, Cove, Eversley, Finchampstead, Headley, Wokingham, and Yateley, only entered Women's teams.

The Hampshire Cricket League Handbook 2016 was used to put the photographs in Part 1 in order.

Note:
Brading, Ryde, Ryde Cavaliers, Shanklin, and Ventnor Cricket Clubs, have all played, or still do play, in the Hampshire or Southern Leagues, but will be found in Part 3, along with Newclose cricket ground.

ALDERHOLT – Recreation Ground

ALDERHOLT CC: The recreation ground here is owned by the Parish Council and caters for several sports.

The first record of cricket being played in Alderholt was in the late 1800s in Alderholt Park. The present Alderholt Cricket Club was founded in 1980.

Located just three miles west of Fordingbridge in East Dorset, Alderholt joined the Hampshire League in 2000.

ALDERSHOT – Guildford Road

ALDERSHOT CC: This pavilion cost £507,000 and was funded by assistance from the Lottery and a grant from Rushmoor Borough Council. It was opened in October 2003 by the Hampshire and England spinner, Shaun Udal. There are two pitches here and the pavilion serves both of them.

Aldershot Cricket Club was formed in 1947. The club was a founding member of the Three Counties League in 1972. In 1993 they joined the larger Thames Valley League in which the First, Second and Third XIs still play. The Fourth, Fifth and Women's XIs play in the Hampshire League.

ALRESFORD – Arlebury Park

This pavilion was built in the 1980s and a second floor was added in 1988. When this photograph was taken in 2006, more building work was in progress, so it will look different now.

In Alresford, at a ceremony on 21 June 2009, a plaque commemorating John Arlott's 20 years of living at the Old Sun was unveiled. This was followed by an inaugural local village cricket competition, with participating teams from Tichborne Park, Old Alresford, Ropley, and Cheriton, for the John Arlott Cup. The plaque can be seen on the side of the Old Sun building.

Tichborne Park Cricket Club use this as a second ground.

ALTON – Jubilee Playing Fields – Pitch I

ALTON CC: The Harry Baker Pavilion. There are two pavilions here, one for each pitch, situated at either end of the playing fields. The Harry Baker Pavilion on Pitch I is used by the Alton Cricket Club in the summer and by local football teams in the winter. The Charles Read Pavilion on Pitch 2 is used by the general public when hiring pitches.

Alton Cricket Club, founded on I May 1869 and nick-named The Brewers, first played at the Municipal Ground, then Anstey Park, and since 1985 here at the Jubilee Playing Fields.

The Alton First XI play in the Southern League, with the Second, Third and Women's XIs in the Hampshire League.

ALTON – Jubilee Playing Fields – Pitch 2

The Charles Read Pavilion.

AMESBURY – Archers Gate

AMESBURY CC: The Centenary Pavilion. This pavilion was opened by the Mayor of Amesbury, Councillor John T Swindlehurst, on 15 August 2015.

Two cricket matches were played near Stonehenge in 1781. In the early 19th century the Stonehenge cricket ground was described as being beautiful and famous. Wiltshire played against Hampshire on it in 1835. Amesbury had a cricket team, and possibly a cricket club, in 1826 but the Amesbury Cricket Club as we know it today was founded around 1890. After the Great War they moved to Countess Road in the town where they stayed until after the Second War when they moved to Bonny Mead Park, as it was originally called. They joined the Hampshire League in 2002. Amesbury Cricket Club moved to Archers Gate from Bonnymead Park in 2015. Archers Gate is named after a Bronze Age man whose skeleton was dug up during excavations for this new development.

AMPFIELD – Recreation Ground

AMPFIELD & NORTH BADDESLEY CC: Ampfield Cricket Club was formed in 1888 and they have played at the 'White Horse Ground' since the early 1900s. They were known as Ampfield Crusaders Cricket Club between 2010 and 2013 before amalgamating with North Baddesley & Knightwood Cricket Club in 2014. See also, NORTH BADDESLEY in Part 2.

Ampfield Parish Council bought the ground when it came on the market in 2002 and, following a landfill project, the usable area of the ground was increased by 40% and a new cricket square was built. A new pavilion was designed and planning permission was approved in 2005 but changes to the landfill tax procedures meant that after installing the base, money ran out and the plans for a new pavilion had to be shelved. The White Horse pub is conveniently situated next to the ground and is used for after-match celebrations.

AMPORT – Grateley Road

AMPORT CC: The grand opening of this pavilion was on the 24 June 1994.

There is a record of a cricket match held on the village green in 1898 between the Ladies and Gentlemen of the Marquis of Winchester's staff. The Marquis was the incumbent of Amport House and he set aside a parcel of land within the confines of his nine-hole golf course at Haydown. It was between the wars that the cricket club moved to Keepers Hill where they played until the early 1980s when the rent was increased and other options were investigated. Then John Peacock purchased the estate and he gave them the ground they now occupy. The old pavilion was taken apart and erected on the new site and was later replaced by the current one.

ANDOVER – Batchelors Barn Road – Pitch 1

ANDOVER CC: This pavilion was built in 1959.

Andover Cricket Club was formed at a public meeting in the White Hart Hotel on 1 April 1863 when forty members subscribed £20 for the necessary gear to be purchased. The Club was established by 1865 with home games being played at Batchelors Barn Road for most of the Club's history. At the end of the 1999 season club cricket in central southern England was re-organised into three primary divisions - Gold, Silver, and Bronze, and the Southern Premier League was born. Andover were invited to join the Gold Division.

The Andover First XI play in the Southern League, with the Second, Third, Fourth and Women's XIs in the Hampshire League.

ANDOVER – Batchelors Barn Road – Pitch 2

This pavilion was opened by the Mayor of Test Valley Council, RJ Bailey, on 25 September 1997.

The Andover Cricket Club Third and Fourth XIs play here on Pitch 2.

ANDOVER – East Anton Sports Ground

THRUXTON CC: This pavilion was opened on 29 April 2016 by the Mayor of Test Valley, Councillor Iris Andersen.

The ground is in the new Augusta Park development to the north of Andover and opened in time for Thruxton Cricket Club to make it their new home in time for the 2016 season. They previously played at the Charlton Sports Centre, the huge Test Valley Council ground that had two cricket tables but no pavilion, which also caters for rugby, football and athletics.

Thruxton are a one-team club that was formed in 1983 by a group of friends and played in the Salisbury & District League until they joined the Hampshire League in 2002.

ASHFORD HILL – Recreation Ground

ASHFORD HILL CC: A wooden pavilion was built in 1963 when Ashford Hill Cricket Club was 'revived'. This current brick-built pavilion replaced it in 1989 and was opened by Margaret Weston, the Mayor of Basingstoke. The pavilion is also home to a pre-school, appropriately named Jiminy Cricket's.

Ashford Hill Cricket Club existed in the 1930s when they played at the original Recreation Ground, which was immediately next door to the present one. They joined the Hampshire League in 1985 and stayed until 1994 when they had a break and re-joined again in 2002.

Two large Lime trees within the boundary have white 'boundary' lines on the trunks about six to eight feet above the ground, a local rule for fours and sixes.

BARTLEY – Busketts Lawn

This is one of the oldest grounds in the New Forest. The last mention of a match involving Bartley Cricket Club in CricketArchive is a New Forest League game against New Milton Third XI on 13 August 1988.

Surrounded by the Forest, this quaint ground at Woodlands was still being used by Langley Manor Cricket Club as a second venue in 2016.

BASHLEY – Bashley Road – Pitch I

BASHLEY (RYDAL) CC: This photograph shows the pavilion as it was 2006. It has since been added to, but this original part remains.

Bashley Cricket Club was formed in 1947 at the Rydal Hotel in New Milton and played at the town's Memorial Ground ('The Rec') as Rydal Cricket Club, They moved to the present ground in 1979, which was voted the Southern League 'Ground of the Year' in 2016.

The Bashley First and Second XIs play in the Southern League, with the Third, Fourth and Fifth XIs in the Hampshire League.

BASHLEY – Bashley Road – Pitch 2

This pavilion was built and opened in 2015.

The Bashley (Rydal) Cricket Club Third and Fourth XIs play here, but the Fourth XI play on the artificial wicket.

BASHLEY – Ballard School

This is the pavilion at the ground, but the changing rooms are in the school buildings.

Set in 32 acres of sports-grounds and gardens, Ballard School has outstanding facilities for most sports including an outdoor heated swimming pool and a multi-purpose sports hall.

Bashley (Rydal) Cricket Club use this school ground for their Fifth XI.

BASINGSTOKE - Malshanger Sports Ground

TADLEY HOBOS CC: The pavilion is 1910 vintage, but the square was laid in 1990.

Malshanger Sports Ground is in the grounds of the Malshanger Estate which is owned by Sir Michael and Lady Colman, the Mustard people.

Tadley Hobos joined the Hampshire League in 1986 but had a break between 2011 and 2014 before returning.

Malshanger was used by Steventon and Deane Cricket Club and the Ferguson Academy Cricket Club in their Hampshire League days.

BASINGSTOKE – May's Bounty

BASINGSTOKE & NORTH HANTS CC: In 1875, a timber and thatch pavilion was built in the centre of the southern side of the ground.

The plaque on this pavilion states 'This pavilion was erected and the ground enlarged and relaid by Colonel John May, the President of Basingstoke & North Hants Cricket Club to inaugurate the New Century January 1 1901'. It was further extended and improved between the 1960s and 1980s. The present club was formed in the Wheatsheaf Inn on 4 May 1865 and their first President was Lt. Col. John May. The earliest recorded game involving a Basingstoke team was in 1817 and the first documented match on the Folly, the present ground, was against Newbury in 1855. There are two grounds here, the second is called Castle Field, and the pavilion serves them both. If things go to plan a new £1.5 million pavilion will replace this one in 2018. The Basingstoke First and Second XIs play in the Southern League, with the Third, Fourth and Fifth XIs in the Hampshire League.

BASINGSTOKE – Newfound

ST MARY'S CC: This pavilion was opened in 2004 and is used for football and cricket.

Newfound is located off the B3400 road opposite The Fox Inn public house and has been a sports ground since the 1930s.

St Mary's Cricket Club is based in the centre of Basingstoke and is made up of church members and their friends. The club have been playing regularly since the mid 1980s and they say they 'aim to play cricket competitively, fairly and in good humour, reflecting the Christian faith that underpins the club'.

BEAULIEU – Palace Lane

BEAULIEU CC: This pavilion here has been extended since 2006 when this photograph was taken, but the basic structure remains.

Cricket was played in the village before Beaulieu Cricket Club was officially formed in 1849. They celebrated 150 years with a match against the MCC in 1999.

Beaulieu have one Saturday side, and a Sunday side that only play Home fixtures.

BEDHAMPTON – Bidbury Mead

BEDHAMPTON MARINERS CC: The Club was founded in 1872 as Stockheath & Bedhampton Cricket Club with home games being played on Stockheath Common. In the 1930s they moved to the present site.

The current club is an amalgamation of the Bedhampton Cricket Club, Mariners Cricket Club and Bedhampton Wednesday Cricket Club.

Bidbury Mead is a large tree-ringed recreation ground which the Cricket Club shares with the Bedhampton Bowls Club.

BENTWORTH – Medstead Road

BENTWORTH CC: This distinctive thatched pavilion has panoramic views of the Hampshire countryside, and a backdrop of Bentworth Hall. It has been preserved for posterity in a painting by Jocelyn Galsworthy.

The ground at Holt End has been used by the village cricket team for over 100 years. The teas are provided by the nearby Sun Inn pub.

BINSTED – Recreation Ground

The plaque in this pavilion says it was opened by Nelson George Clements on Saturday 25 July 1992. The Binsted Parish Council also use the pavilion as their office.

Rowledge Cricket Club Third XI use this ground for their Hampshire League fixtures, and Binsted Cricket Club, and others, use the ground for Friendly games.

BISHOPS WALTHAM – Albany Road

BISHOPS WALTHAM CC: This pavilion was built in 2000 by life-member Ron Harvey when the Club moved from their previous ground at Hoe Road at the start of the 2001 season.

Bishops Waltham Cricket Club was founded in about 1770. See also, the Hoe Road pavilion in Part 2.

BLACKFIELD – Queen Elizabeth II Recreation Ground

The QE2 Pavilion is the newest of the Fawley Parish Council facilities. It was opened in Spring 2008 and was jointly funded by the Parish Council, New Forest District Council, Hampshire County Council and the Football Foundation.

Hythe & Dibden Cricket Club use this as a second ground.

BOSCOMBE – Kings Park

LYTCHETT CC: The Kings Park pavilion was opened in 1904. Additions were made to it in 1929 and some further alterations were made in 1948, so the building today is an amalgamation of several different periods of history.

Kings Park has three cricket squares, all served by this grandiose pavilion which has its own cafe. The park was previously known as Common No 59. To mark the Coronation of Edward VII the Council decided on 20 May 1902 to re-name it Kings Park.

Dorset side Lytchett Cricket Club used this ground in 2016 while improvements were being made to their own ground. Parley Cricket Club use Kings Park as a second ground.

BOTLEY – The Recreation Ground

IBM SOUTH HANTS CC and KNOWLE VILLAGE CC: IBM South Hants Cricket Club is an amalgamation of the IBM Cosham and IBM Havant Cricket Clubs who combined in the 1970s and called themselves IBM Portsmouth. They then became IBM South Hants Cricket Club and played at the IBM Havant plant in Langstone Road until 1992 when their playing fields were built upon. They re-located to the Company ground at Hursley for their Hampshire League games but the Hursley club started a Second XI and in 2013 they moved to Shedfield - New Place, where the facilities were unsuitable for the higher reaches of the League so they had to move again, to Botley in 2015. Knowle Cricket Club re-located here in 2016 when their local council withdrew support at their previous home at Knowle village green. The Hampshire Bowman Cricket Club, formed in 2005 also play here, but only play Sunday Friendlies.

BOURNEMOUTH – Chapel Gate – Pitch 1

BOURNEMOUTH CC: This new complex was fully opened by October 1989. The official opening ceremony was conducted by the former Prime Minister Ted Heath MP in April 1991.

The Bournemouth Cricket Club history before 1930 is vague, but it is known that they existed long before then under various guises. The Bournemouth Cricket Sports Club was formed in 1930 and until 1987 operated from a site in Kinson. The playing sections were primarily cricket, hockey, rugby, and squash. In 1987 Bournemouth Sports Club disposed of the Kinson site and bought the 65-acre Chapel Gate site from Barclays Bank. There are now three cricket pitches here, but Pitch 3 has an artificial wicket and no real pavilion.

The Bournemouth First XI play in the Southern League, with the Second, Fourth and Fifth XIs in the Hampshire League.

BOURNEMOUTH – Chapel Gate – Pitch 2

The pavilion on Pitch 2 was constructed thanks to a £50,000 grant from the ECB's Community Club Development Fund and was opened by the local Member of Parliament, Chris Chope.

The old Nursery End sight-screens from Lord's also found their way here.

BOURNEMOUTH – Kinson Manor

SUTTONERS CC: Cricket was banned at Kinson Manor in 2011 because stray balls were considered a danger to the public. The problem seems to have been overcome and Suttoners have returned here from their temporary home at Slades Farm.

Suttoners Cricket Club was founded in 1967.

Cricket used to be played on the Kinson village green which has now become a residential area, with Wicket Road being named to mark its previous life.

BOURNEMOUTH – Littledown Centre

This complex was opened on 15 March 1989 by the Mayor of Bournemouth, Jacqueline 'Jacky' Harris. A life-long cricket fan, she was awarded the MBE in 2002.

The Littledown Centre is situated within 47 acres of park land and is a modern multi-use sports centre.

Christchurch Cricket Club and Parley Cricket Club both use this as a second ground.

BOURNEMOUTH – Wallisdown Recreation Ground

DORSET INDIANS CC: This ground is the home of Branksome Cricket Club who were formed in 1977 and teamed-up with Parkstone Cricket Club in 2013. They play in the Dorset League.

The Hampshire connection is provided by Dorset Indians Cricket Club, which was founded in 2015 and made this their home ground in 2016.

BRAMLEY – Clift Meadow Park

The pavilion here was completed in July 1994 and cost £66,000. It was extended around 2005.

Since this photograph was taken in 2008 a second building called Brocas Hall has been built alongside it. Some of the best known facilities in the village have been bequested by generous residents. The Clift Meadow is land given in perpetuity to the village of Bramley under the wills of William and John Clift, farmers who owned much of the land around the village. They also gifted the Village Hall to the community.

Bramley is an historical village, built on the Roman Road that ran from Silchester to Chichester.

Old Basing Cricket Club use Clift Meadow as a second ground.

BRAMSHAW – Roundhills

BRAMSHAW CC: The previous pavilion was replaced in 1970 by this one which was opened in 1971 by Lady Crosthwaite-Eyre, the wife of Oliver who was Member of Parliament for the New Forest until 1968.

Bramshaw Cricket Club was founded in 1877. The Club was revived in 1920 after stopping in 1914 because of the Great War. Then the Second World War intervened and the Club had to be revived again in 1948 with £10.3s.11d in the bank, and a further £100 as settlement for War Damage!

In 2016 Bramshaw Cricket Club came to an agreement with Nomansland Cricket Club which would see them being responsible for their ground, and the re-naming of Nomansland as Bramshaw Third XI.

BRAMSHILL – Police College

This ground was laid out in about 1810 and in 1823 a Hampshire XI played against England here.

Bramshill House was built between 1605 and 1612 for Edward, Lord Zouche of Harringworth. In 1960 the estate became the permanent home of the principal police staff training college in the UK.

This photograph was taken in 2006 when the Police College was still in residence. By 2016 the estate was privately owned and plans were in hand to demolish this pavilion and build a new one on the opposite side of the field.

Hartley Wintney Cricket Club use this as a second ground.

BRANSGORE – The New Recreation Ground

BRANSGORE CC: This pavilion was opened in 2003 by Hampshire's James Tomlinson.

This village sports ground, big enough for four football pitches, lies at the far south-western edge of the New Forest National Park, just inside the Hampshire border with Dorset.

Bransgore Cricket Club in its current incarnation, dates from the 1970s when they played on the recreation ground across the road from the current one.

Bransgore joined the Hampshire League in 2003 when they joined the New Forest Division.

BREAMORE – Breamore Marsh

BREAMORE CC: This lovely old thatched pavilion was built in 1902, but there is a lack of 'facilities' that prevents the club from progressing from the Regional Divisions of the Hampshire League. Breamore are not alone in having trouble with this rule. Nearby Godshill have the same problem and it contributed to the failure of Swan Green Cricket Club, which is a shame as these grounds are loved by players and public alike.

It is thought that cricket was first played in the village on the lawn in front of Breamore House which was built in 1583. The building underwent minor changes in the 18th century, and major restoration after a fire in 1856. The history of the Club remains sketchy, but cricket has been played at the Marsh, which is listed as a Site of Special Scientific Interest, for over 100 years. There is no bar in the pavilion, but the Bat and Ball Inn is conveniently nearby.

BROCKENHURST – Balmer Lawn Hotel

BROCKENHURST CC: The Hampshire Chronicle mentioned a match between Brockenhurst and Southampton in 1797 and another later the same year against Portsmouth White Swan Club. In 1870, and probably earlier, cricket was played at Brockenhurst Park which was said to have one of the best pitches in England. It was owned by John Morant, whose family owned much of Brockenhurst and its surrounds. Sometime between 1906 and 1914 the Club moved to the current picturesque ground in front of the Balmer Lawn Hotel, which they lease from the Forestry Commission, and have remained there ever since.

The hotel was built in the mid-1800s but a major fire in the early 1970s changed the aspect of the hotel when the original roof was replaced with the mansard-style one of today.

BROUGHTON – Sports Field

BROUGHTON CC: The sports field and pavilion, which was built in 1974, is managed by the Parish Council and rented for use by Broughton's football and cricket clubs.

Broughton Cricket Club was established on 7 December 1865 at the Greyhound Inn, Broughton. The 150-year anniversary celebration was held at the very same place on 7 December 2015.

BURLEY – Burley School Green

BURLEY CC: The Vernon Simmonds Pavilion. In 1962 the idea of a new pavilion was tabled, but it took another 12 years to become a reality and this pavilion opened in 1975. It was extensively modified in 2011, mostly on the inside, but partly on the outside, since this photograph was taken in 2006. Much of the cost was met from a bequest from former Battle of Britain pilot, Sqn Ldr Vernon Churchill Simmonds, who died on 23 February 2005.

There are few early records of Burley Cricket Club. It is known that the club was founded in 1875 when cricket was played on Burley Lawn. Much like today, it was the ponies that kept the grass cropped. The earliest picture in the club's possession shows the Burley Cricket XI of 1897. It was not until 1900, when the Rev. AB Cummins became vicar of Burley, that a proper club was formed. 1912 saw the club move to its present location on Burley School Green. In 1940 the club fielded just one team due to lack of players caused by World War II, but play continued unlike during the 1914-18 war.

BURRIDGE – Burridge Sports Ground

BURRIDGE CC: This pavilion opened in 1996 at the ground that is now known as 'The Ridge'.

Burridge Cricket Club was founded on 1 January 1968. This sports ground was initiated in 1986 when Burridge Sports and Social Club purchased the 10.5 acres of farmland. The Cricket Club was closely involved in the project, and itself financed the laying of the cricket square on the ground, which led to the first games being played here in 1990. In the early years the ground required much work, and temporary changing rooms were used. By 1997, with the new pavilion built, the Club was awarded the prestigious Stan Foster award for the most improved ground.

The Burridge First XI play in the Southern League, with the Second, Third and Fourth XIs in the Hampshire League.

BURRIDGE – Recreation Ground

This is the original ground adjacent to the Burridge Sports and Social Club to which the Cricket Club's 150 or so members belong. Burridge Cricket Club now use 'the Rec' as a second ground.

In 2006 the Club was strengthened by the move of the former New Forest Ladies team to Burridge, where they now play in the Hampshire Cricket League Women's Division.

CADNAM – Lamb's Corner

CADNAM CC: Cadnam Cricket Club was established in 1880. They moved to Lamb's Corner from their previous ground on land owned by their President at the time, Mr Dalrymple. That ground was near the nursery and the Haywain pub. The two previous grounds before that were behind pubs also. This one is near the Sir John Barleycorn, but like most clubs today they have their own bar. The first match to be played here was in August 1956.

Cadnam run three teams in the Hampshire League and use Minstead as an out-ground.

CALMORE – Loperwood Park

CALMORE SPORTS CC: Jimmy Gray, the former Hampshire County Cricket Club opening batsman, opened Loperwood Park and the pavilion on 17 May 1981.

Calmore Cricket Club was formed in 1913 but their first match was on 13 April 1914. Their first ground was at Hopkin's Field off Water Lane in Totton near the Coopers Arms pub, now known as the Players Arms, before moving to Calmore in the mid-1930s. Cricket stopped in 1939 and after the war they played on the famous Horseshoe Ground at Paultons until 1951 before Paultons Cricket Club re-formed. Then they moved back to the King George V Ground in Calmore for the next thirty years.

The Calmore First XI play in the Southern League, with the Second, Third and Fourth XIs in the Hampshire League.

CALMORE – King George V Playing Fields

This ground was left by a local farmer to the village of Calmore for recreational use. It was first used by Calmore Cricket Club when they moved here from their original ground in Totton. After the war they played in Paultons Park before returning here in 1951 and staying until 1981 when Loperwood Park opened. This was their main ground and tea was taken in the Village Hall in Pauletts Lane. It is still used today as an out-ground for their Third and Fourth XIs.

CHANDLER'S FORD – Knightwood Leisure Centre

KNIGHTS VALLEY CC: The Knightwood Leisure Centre opened in 2003 and is a multi-purpose facility catering for many sports and pastimes. It is run by Valley Leisure, a charitable organisation that was formed in 1990 to promote the well-being of the residents of the Test Valley.

Knights Valley Cricket Club was officially formed in the winter of 2010. It was conceived in the garden of the Cleveland Bay pub. The name was dreamt up by Sam Fielder, and is an amalgamation of two areas of Chandler's Ford, Knightwood and Valley Park.

Valley Park was home for three great cricketers – Malcolm Marshall, Gordon Greenidge, and Desmond Haynes.

Knights Valley use Knightwood as their home ground. Ampfield & North Baddesley Cricket Club use it as their second ground.

47

CHAWTON

CHAWTON CC: Founded in 1883, Chawton Cricket Club has an idyllic setting close to the church of St Nicholas, Jane Austen's Chawton House, and the Greyfriars pub.

It is believed that Chawton Cricket Club have always played at this ground.

CHERITON

This pavilion was opened by John Arlott on 28 April 1963.

Cheriton Cricket Club only play Friendly cricket and are renowned for their teas. An additional attraction is the Flowerpots pub and the brewery across the road!

The Hampshire Wayfarers Cricket Club use the Flowerpots as their clubhouse. Their aim is to play all-day games against quality sides at quality venues and their fixture card reflects this. Their motto 'Ubi Peregrinari, Omnes Ludere, Omnia Bibere' is said to translate as 'Travel Everywhere, Play Everyone, Drink Everything'.

Easton & Martyr Worthy Cricket Club use Cheriton as a second ground.

CHRISTCHURCH – Grange Road

EAST CHRISTCHURCH CC: This was previously known as the BAE Systems Ground, and was home to the BAE Systems Cricket Club until 2013.

There is no pavilion at the ground. Players have to get changed here at the East Christchurch Sports Club.

East Christchurch Cricket Club use Grange Road as their main ground. Bransgore Cricket Club use it as a second ground.

CHRISTCHURCH – Hurn Bridge Sports & Social Club

CHRISTCHURCH CC: The Hurn Bridge Sports & Social Club building was opened by Councillor Eric Spreadbury in 1984.

It is currently sponsored by a tarmacadam company and is known as the MA Hart Stadium.

Christchurch Cricket Club is based here and share the facilities with Christchurch Football Club, Bournemouth Football Association, and the Dorset Cricket Centre.

The Christchurch First XI play in the Dorset League, with the Second and Third XIs in the Hampshire League.

COLDEN COMMON – Colden Common Park

COLDEN COMMON CC: This pavilion was officially opened at a ceremony on 25 April 1999 and the first cricket match was played here in May 2000.

The Parish Council bought 17 acres of farmland on the eastern edge of the village in 1996 which led to a £400,000 sport and leisure facility for the local population. Colden Common Park was opened in April 1997. Encouraged by the Sports Council, Colden Common Parish Council applied for a Lottery grant and at the end of 1997 was awarded over £260,000 towards a pavilion and a bowling green.

COMPTON

COMPTON CC: This West Sussex club has two pavilions but one of them is the tea-room. This photograph shows the changing room. A new tea room was being constructed when this picture was taken in 2009.

See also, COMPTON in Part 2.

COMPTON & SHAWFORD – Memorial Playing Fields

COMPTON & CHANDLER'S FORD CC: The Jubilee Pavilion opened in 2003.

Compton & Shawford Cricket Club have been going since the 1920s and played at Compton Street on a field behind the school and church. After the war this playing field on Compton Down was given to the parish and the Club established itself here. At the end of 1995 they joined up with Chandler's Ford Cricket Club and became Compton & Chandler's Ford Cricket Club. See also, the old pavilion in Part 2.

COVE – Southwood Playing Fields

COVE CC: This is the second ground which opened in 1993 and is used by the Cove Cricket Club women's team.

Cove run five men's teams on Saturday's but it is only the Women's XI that plays in the Hampshire League. See also, COVE – Grasmere Road in Part 2.

COWPLAIN – Recreation Ground

This building is known as the Cowplain Activity Centre and caters for all sorts. It was opened on the 25 February 1983 by the Mayor of Havant Councillor CE Ladbrook. It is one of the many Community Centres run by the Havant Borough Council.

Havant Cricket Club use Cowplain for their Hampshire League side. Waterlooville Cricket Club also use it as a second ground.

CRONDALL – Hook Meadow

This pavilion, photographed in 2008, was opened in 1980 and is shared by the Crondall Bowls Club and the Cricket Club. It was totally renovated in 2014 after the roof was blown off during the 2013 gales.

In 1947-1948 the Parish Council hoped to obtain Hook Meadow for building council houses. Mr Beddington, owner of the land, objected strongly to this and would not allow building of any sort on his land. A Parish meeting was convened and the result was in favour of it being turned into a recreation ground as a memorial to the village people who served in the armed forces during the war. Mr Beddington agreed to let it on a 60 year lease at 24 shillings per year.

Odiham & Greywell Cricket Club use this as a second ground. Farnham Cricket Club used it during their brief stay in the Hampshire League between 2006 and 2008.

CURDRIDGE – Reading Room Lane

CURDRIDGE CC: This pavilion dates from 1984. The previous pavilion, known as the 'Nissen Hut' was said to have cost 60 shillings to erect.

Curdridge Cricket Club was formed in 1853 and moved to this ground in 1885.

The Curdridge Reading Room and Recreation Ground dates from 1884 and is a charity run for the benefit of all the inhabitants of Curdridge and their neighbours in Curbridge.

DAMERHAM – The Cricket Field

DAMERHAM CC: Damerham Cricket Club is known to have existed since 1832. They moved to this ground around 1915 from a site off Cornpits Lane in the south of the village.

The Compass Inn is only a few yards from the pavilion and provides an ideal retreat for after-match celebrations, or otherwise.

The village is under the care of the New Forest District Council, but is not in the New Forest National Park. Nor is it in Dorset or Wiltshire, though both are very close.

DENMEAD – King George V Playing Field

DENMEAD CC: This pavilion was opened in 2005, and was built as joint venture with the local football team. The Denmead Cricket Club crest shows a foundation date of 1903.

The King George's Fields Foundation was set up as a national scheme in March 1936 to commemorate the death of His Royal Highness King George V. In Denmead this playing field in Ashling Park Road was part of the scheme. Denmead Cricket Club joined the Hampshire League in 1976 and have always used this ground.

DINTON

DINTON CC: This pavilion was opened by former Salisbury MP Lord Margadale in 1982. It was built mainly by club members, led by the then club captain John Woolley. It is now managed by the Dinton Recreation Ground Charitable Trust, and after the formation of Dinton Rugby Club in 2015 the pavilion is now used all year around for the two different sports.

The village is nine miles west of Salisbury in Wiltshire and the cricket club was first established here in 1921.

Dinton have two Saturday teams that play in the Hampshire Cricket League, a Wednesday team, and a Sunday Friendly team.

DONNINGTON – The Dell

DONNINGTON CC: Donnington Cricket Club was founded in 1890. They play at Donnington village recreation ground, affectionately called The Dell, near Newbury in Berkshire. In 2015 the club celebrated its 125th anniversary.

Donnington have a League team on a Saturday and a Sunday team which plays a mixture of competitive and prestigious Friendly matches.

EASEBOURNE – Rotherfield Sports Grounds

EASEBOURNE CC: The Club's minute book records the Rotherfield was in use in 1938, but the Club is older than that. CricketArchive has a match between Easebourne and Eton Ramblers on 1 June 1935.

There was a second pavilion here that had fallen into disrepair when this photograph was taken in 2008.

Easebourne Cricket Club in West Sussex have a Saturday XI playing in the Hampshire League and a Sunday team playing Friendlies.

EAST TYTHERLEY

East Tytherley Cricket Club is over 130 years old. CricketArchive has a scorecard from a game played against Romsey Social at Alma Road, Romsey, on 24 April 1880. They withdrew from the Hampshire League in 2012, but still compete in the Border League and play a few Friendlies, so their opponents can share the delights of the splendid 17th century Star Inn, which is located right next to the ground, after they've used this very pretty pavilion.

Old Tauntonians & Romsey Cricket Club use this as a second ground.

EAST WOODHAY – Malverleys

EAST WOODHAY CC: East Woodhay Cricket Club was established in 1856. After some time being linked with Woolton Hill Cricket Club and playing near Woolton Rectory, they moved to this ground in the village of East End in the 1920s.

East Woodhay have two teams in the Hampshire League and play Friendlies on Sunday. The midweek side is known as the Woodhay Woodpeckers and they play in the Downs Cricket League.

The ground was voted the Hampshire League 'Ground of the Year' in 2014.

EASTLEIGH – Doncaster Farm

RIVERSIDE CC and SPORTING WESSEX CC: This Eastleigh Borough Council ground is located directly opposite the Cricketers Arms public house. It is part of North Stoneham Park, an historic area that includes the Stoneham War Shrine in Avenue Park and several sports grounds, A planned housing development meant that 2016 was its final year. Riverside Cricket Club and Sporting Wessex Cricket Club both used this as their main ground. Riverside was formed in 2008 and started in 2009 as an Evening League side playing at Riverside Park, before joining the Hampshire League in 2011. Sporting Wessex started as a football team in 2002 called Spar-Tec Wessex, taking the name from a Hamble-based boat-riggers who were the original sponsors. They changed the name to Sporting and started a cricket team 2013, and they will set up a new home at Wide Lane in 2017.

EASTLEIGH – University Ground

SOUTHAMPTON COMMUNITY CC: Wide Lane Sports Grounds were opened in 2005 by sports broadcaster John Inverdale. The University has invested £4.3 million in the 76-acre facility in partnership with Eastleigh Borough Council and the Football Foundation. There are four cricket pitches here and the pavilion shown is the one at the northern end.

The University fielded five teams in 2016, but none of them play in the Hampshire or Southern Leagues.

Southampton Community Cricket Club use Wide Lane as their main ground and Millbrook Recreation Ground, which does not have a pavilion any more, as their second ground.

IBM Hursley, and Trojans Cricket Club use Wide Lane as a second ground.

EASTON & MARTYR WORTHY – David Roth Cricket Ground

EASTON & MARTYR WORTHY CC: With financial help from the National Lottery and Easton village, this pavilion was built and opened in 2010.

David Roth was the first President of the Club between 1946 and 1959 and his son John has been President since then. The ground is also known as Cocket's Mead.

The earliest reference to Easton Cricket Club was in 1903, but like many clubs, it disbanded between 1941 and 1946 when it was re-formed. At this time they amalgamated with the Martyr Worthy Cricket Club and the first record of the combined team was an away match against Old Alresford on 13 July 1946.

ELLINGHAM – Picket Post

ELLINGHAM CC: There are now two cricket squares here, and the pavilion serves them both.

The Club was founded in 1837 as Somerley Cricket Club and played at Somerley House prior to their move to the present ground. The Somerley Club was re-formed in 1948 and in 1963 they made the move to Picket Post and changed their name to Ellingham Cricket Club.

EMSWORTH – Hollybank Recreation Ground

Portsdown Cricket Club used this ground in 1977 for their Hampshire League games.

Bedhampton Mariners Cricket Club currently use Hollybank as an out-ground for their Third and Fourth XIs.

EMSWORTH – Recreation Ground

EMSWORTH CC: This pavilion was built in the 1980s.

Cricket in Emsworth has been played at the same ground, Cold Harbour Lawn, since 1761. The ground was re-named Emsworth Recreation Ground in 1909 and is the current home of Emsworth Cricket Club which was founded in 1811.

Emsworth celebrated their Bicentenary with a match against the MCC.

EVERSLEY – Eversley Cross Green

EVERSLEY CC: This pavilion dates from at least the 1930s as it was used to house two evacuee families during the war. Cricket has been played here since Monday 2 July 1787 when 'The Gentlemen of Warfield played The Gentlemen of Eversley, for 10 guineas a side, with wickets to be pitched at 10 o'clock'. The notice added that there would be 'Good entertainment at the ground'.

Adjacent to the ground is The Frog and Wicket pub, which sits on the Three Castles Path, a route travelled by King John as he journeyed to give his seal to the Magna Carta at Runnymede in 1215.

Eversley Cricket Club have four men's Saturday teams who play in the Thames Valley League, and a women's team in the Hampshire League.

EVERSLEY – Eversley New Ground

The Eversley Indoor Cricket Centre opened in January 2010, and the first games played on the New Ground were in the summer of 2010.

EXBURY

EXBURY CC and CAMELOT CC: Lionel de Rothschild moved to Exbury in 1912 and in 1919 he purchased the Exbury Estate and set about creating the world-famous gardens. The Exbury Social Club was originally built for the many staff who were employed to construct the gardens. It is still a Members Club, of which the Cricket Club is a part. Exbury Cricket Club are a one-team Club so they are able to share the ground with Camelot.

Camelot Cricket Club was formed in 1965 at the Camelot Press printing company in Shirley, Southampton and joined the Hampshire League in 2002. Sadly, both clubs folded at the end of the 2016 season.

FAIR OAK – Lapstone Park

FAIR OAK CC: This multi-purpose pavilion was opened on 10 January 1998 by Rajesh Maru the former Middlesex and Hampshire County Cricket Club spinner, and is run by Horton Heath Parish Council.

The present Fair Oak Cricket Club was founded in 1947 and has exclusive use of this ground after playing many years at Bishopstoke Recreation Ground. With four Saturday sides they need out-grounds and in 2016 used both Shedfield Recreation Ground and Twyford's Hunter Park.

The Fair Oak First XI play in the Southern League, with the Second, Third and Fourth XIs in the Hampshire League.

FAREHAM – Bath Lane Recreation Ground

FAREHAM & CROFTON CC: The original pavilion here was built in 1904 for £500. This clubhouse was built in 1978. In the winter of 2014 the pavilion underwent a full refurbishment, with a new block being added to the left side of the old pavilion. There are two pitches here and the pavilion serves them both.

Fareham Cricket Club was founded in 1882. Crofton Cricket Club was formed by amalgamating the Stubbington and Lee-on-Solent Cricket Clubs in 1947. Crofton joined up with Fareham in 1990.

St James Casuals Cricket Club were founded in 1938 and played at Botley and Buriton before coming here in 2010. They just play Sunday Friendly cricket.

FARLEY – Coronation Field

FARLEY CC: By 1960 Bill Goldfinch, the man who secretly built a glider in Colditz during World War 2, had prepared plans for a pavilion that was to be built voluntarily by members of the football and cricket clubs. Building materials cost £682. On 24 June 1961 George Fanshawe opened the pavilion.

Earliest records suggest Farley Cricket Club has existed since 1866 and they played on various make-shift grounds around the village.

Also known as the Farley Fox Playing Field, Coronation Field is so named because it was bought from the public subscription of villagers to commemorate the Coronation Year of 1953. The purchase was finalised on 16 February 1954 and the ground was opened by George Fanshawe, Lord Lieutenant of Wiltshire.

FAWLEY – Waterside Sports & Social Club

FAWLEY CC: The changing rooms are part of the Social Club. This neat little pavilion is out on the field.

Formed on 10 January 1927 as the American Gulf & West Indies Oil Company (AGWI) Cricket Club, their original home ground was in Fawley, but they moved to Netley View in 1929. Around 1936 Esso bought out AGWI and the present club at Holbury was bought. The first game of cricket was played there in June 1937. The club was called Esso Cricket Club from about 1944 but around 1954 they amalgamated with Fawley Cricket Club to form Esso (Fawley) Cricket Club. In 2003 the refinery handed over the club and grounds to the members and the team name reverted to Fawley Cricket Club. They also use the school pitch next door for the Third XI home matches. The Fawley First XI play in the Southern League, with the Second and Third XIs in the Hampshire League.

FERNDOWN – Dolmans Farm

FERNDOWN WAYFARERS CC: The Ferndown Wayfarers Cricket and Sports Club ground at Dolmans Farm has two grass cricket squares.

The Ferndown Cricket Club and Wayfarers Cricket Club merged in March 2010 to form the present Club. They have four Saturday League teams, three in the Hampshire League and one, their Second XI, in the Dorset League.

FERNDOWN – King George V Playing Fields

WINTON CC: This pavilion opened in 1962. It was improved and added to, and the extended pavilion was opened by golfer Peter Alliss on 8 September 1985.

The ground was then the home of Ferndown RBL Cricket Club, who became Ferndown Strollers Cricket Club and have since moved on. It is now home to Winton Cricket Club who use this as their first choice venue. They share the pavilion with the Ferndown Bowls Club which was founded in 1962.

The old pavilion here is used by the local Football Club.

FINCHAMPSTEAD – Leas Ground

FINCHAMPSTEAD CC: Finchampstead Park was established around 1930.

The Leas Ground is adjacent to the Memorial Ground and is used by the Finchampstead Women's team in the Hampshire League.

Finchampstead Cricket Club was officially founded in 1857, but archives suggest it may have been 50 years before that. The Club is renowned as being one of Berkshire's best. The First XI play in the Home Counties Premier League and their other four Saturday League Teams are in the Thames Valley League.

The main pitch at the Memorial Ground has been used by Hampshire CCC for Second XI games.

FISHBOURNE – Fishbourne Centre

SALTHILL CC: The Fishbourne Centre is the result of an extensive renovation of the former Fishbourne Club which was made possible by generous support from The Big Lottery Fund, West Sussex County Council, Chichester District Council, local organisations, and the residents of Fishbourne. The Centre looks out onto 17 acres of playing fields which include cricket and football pitches, tennis courts, a croquet lawn and a bowling green.

Salthill Cricket Club is based in Fishbourne and this has been their main ground since 2007.

Solent Rangers Cricket Club use this as a second ground.

FROXFIELD – King George V Recreation Ground

FROXFIELD CC: The King George V Memorial Hall. This new pavilion and village hall opened in 2002.

Two grounds, at Stoner Hill and Rings Green, are recalled by older villagers as being used before the Great War. This ground at High Cross has been the home of Froxfield Cricket since 1946. It is thought that the Club was established in the late 1800s but like many others they folded in 1914. They were revived about 1922 when the ground was at The Slade, where they played until 1939. The AGM on 27 March 1940 agreed to try to carry on playing. They shared the ground with the Searchlight Battery that was stationed in the village, but not much more cricket was played there until after the war.

GODSHILL

GODSHILL CC: Godshill Cricket Club moved to this ground in 1951.

The village cricket pitch is half a mile east of Godshill village, surrounded by the gorse and heather of the New Forest. Nothing exists of the previous ground which was close to the Fighting Cocks public house. The pub is where tea was taken in the 1970s.

The lack of 'facilities', and an outfield that is given back to the Forest wildlife after stumps, means that promotion to the County Divisions of the Hampshire League is barred.

GOSPORT – Privett Park – Pitch 1

GOSPORT BOROUGH CC: The Clock Tower Pavilion. This factory-built pavilion was delivered in a day and finishing work took just nine weeks. It was opened in 2008. The original Clock Tower Pavilion was vandalised and burned down on 21 May 2005.

Privett Park opened in 1937. It has three cricket squares and two pavilions. The second pavilion is used for games played on pitches 2 and 3.

Gosport Borough Cricket Club, who use the main pitch, was founded in 1966 by amalgamating Gosport Amateurs Cricket Club and Gosport Cricket Club.

The Gosport Borough First XI play in the Southern League, with the Second, Third and Fourth XIs in the Hampshire League.

GOSPORT – Privett Park – Pitches 2 and 3

CHALLENGERS GOSPORT CC: This is the pavilion that is used for the other two pitches at Privett Park.

Challengers Gosport Cricket Club use Privett Park as their main ground. Challengers are relative newcomers to the Hampshire League, joining in 2015.

Gosport Borough Cricket Club use Pitches 2 and 3 for their Third and Fourth XIs.

GREAT DURNFORD

GREAT DURNFORD CC: It is believed that Jim Powell, who was the Captain at the time, was the builder of the original pavilion (hut), so it is at least seventy years old. It has been extended twice since then. The first time was around 1984 when the double glazing went in, and then about four or five years ago when a new equipment area was installed.

At this Wiltshire club they say - 'Nestled in the beautiful Woodford Valley the Great Durnfordians play cricket with a good heart, friendly spirit, and above all, to have fun. When we do well, we wonder whether we can get the Black Horse pub to open early, and when we don't do so well we wonder whether we can get the Black Horse to open early'!

HALE – Hatchett Green

In 1927 a public meeting was held in Hale School to discuss raising funds to build a village hall. By the end of 1929 sufficient funds had been raised and in 1931 a plot of land was purchased adjoining the village green. It was officially opened on 16 February 1932. In 1936 electricity was installed, but it was not until 1950 that a piped water supply was available. More recently the hall has undergone further refurbishment and now has a fully equipped kitchen. Redlynch & Hale Cricket Club use this ground for their Third XI.

HAMBLE – College Playing Field

FRIENDS CC: The Roy Underdown Pavilion. The pavilion was built and opened in 1995. Roy Underdown was the Chairman of the Parish Council who was elected 17 times, achieving the status of being the Council's longest-serving Chairman.

The land here became available following the loss of the College of Air Training sports field in the mid 1990s when the Council leased part of the former airfield to form the College Playing Fields.

Friends Cricket Club, formed in 2012, are what it says on the tin! A group of friends who loved cricket and formed a team to play in the Southampton Evening League and the Hampshire League.

HAMBLE – Folland Park

FOLLANDS (HAMBLE) CC: The Folland Aircraft company was formed in Hamble in 1937 and the Sports Club started soon after.

Follands (Hamble) Cricket Club have almost returned to their original Follands Cricket Club name after numerous name-changes over the last 40 years.

The 'Gate Guard' at the ground is a Folland Gnat, well-known for its role with the famous Red Arrows aerobatic display-team in the past.

HAMBLEDON – Judges Meadow

This pitch is in the grounds of Leydene House, East Meon.

Leydene House was commissioned as HMS *Mercury* on 16 August 1941 as a shore establishment for the Royal Navy.

Hambledon Cricket Club use Judges Meadow as a second ground.

HAMBLEDON – Ridge Meadow

HAMBLEDON CC: The pavilion before this one was opened on 22 June 1969 by the then President of the MCC, Ronnie Aird, but suffered a major fire on 9 September 2007. It was rebuilt and this picture was taken in 2010.

Hambledon Cricket Club was officially founded in 1750 and relocated to Ridge Meadow in the 1780s. Originally based at Broadhalfpenny Down, the Club earned a reputation as the 'cradle of cricket'. Today the old ground and the equally famous Bat and Ball pub across the road are places of pilgrimage for cricket lovers around the world. See Part 2.

Hambledon First XI play in the Southern League, with their Second and Third XIs in the Hampshire League.

HARTLEY WINTNEY – The Cricket Green

HARTLEY WINTNEY CC: This pavilion was opened by Councillor Peter Carr on 7 April 1990.

The Cricket Green is one of the oldest cricket grounds in England. Hartley Wintney Cricket Club was founded in 1770 and have always played here. In those early days they changed in The Cricketers pub that overlooks the ground. Later, and until 1954, they used a railway carriage and then a pavilion was built that lasted until it was destroyed by fire in 1985. Another was built but that only survived until the great storm of 1987.

Hartley Wintney First XI play in the Southern League, with their Second and Third XIs in the Hampshire League.

HAVANT – Havant Park

HAVANT CC: The local newspaper referred to the 'handsome pavilion on the new recreation ground' that was finished in May 1890. A match between Portsmouth Town Council and the Havant Local Board celebrated the event. It was renovated in 1975.

Havant Cricket Club was founded in the 1880s and around 1905 they started ground-sharing with the town Hockey Club. The Hampshire 2nd XI have played here twice.

Havant First and Second XIs play in the Southern League. The Third XI play their Hampshire League games at Cowplain.

HAYLING ISLAND – Hayling Park

HAYLING ISLAND CC and SOLENT RANGERS CC: There are two cricket squares here and the pavilion, built in 1981, serves both. The pavilion also doubles up as the Hayling Island Community Centre.

Hayling Island Cricket Club was founded in 1920.

The first Hampshire Cricket League fixture took place at Hayling Park on 28 April 1973 between Hayling Island CC and Portsmouth & Southsea CC.

Solent Rangers Cricket Club joined the Hampshire League in 2014.

HEADLEY – Playing Fields

HEADLEY CC: The Margery Wheatley Pavilion. The Thackeray Pavilion served the Club until this one opened in September 1996. Margery Wheatley was the wife of Bill Wheatley who donated significant funds to the new project. This is also the headquarters of the Headley Sports Association which was formed to manage the building on behalf of all the user-clubs.

Headley Cricket Club was founded in 1872 and played in the Glebe field behind the Holly Bush pub until 1954 when they moved here. Mr and Mrs RCB Thackeray gave the village the present sports field together with a wooden pavilion. Reg Thackeray was the Club President at the time. The Headley Club currently play in the l'Anson League, but they have a women's team in the Hampshire League.

HEDGE END – Turnpike Playing Fields

The Turnpike Playing Fields opened in 1991. The pavilion, which opened in 1995, is a community centre run by Hedge End Town Council and is used by local cricket and football clubs.

Old Netley & Highfield Cricket Club and Totton & Eling Cricket Club both use this as a second ground.

HERRIARD – Herriard Green

HERRIARD CC: The Owen White Pavilion.

In 1999 planning approval was granted to create a new sports field in the village. Following a major funding project this ground was officially opened in 2011. Herriard Cricket Club moved across the road from the Old Ground to this brand new ground at Nashes Field, which they then re-named Herriard Green.

HERRIARD – Old Ground

In 1978 JL Jervoise, the President of the Club, opened this pavilion to serve both football and cricket.

Herriard Sports Club was established in 1884 and began life at Glebe Field. In 1946 the football team moved to a field behind the school, sharing it with the local livestock. In 1948, the cows moved out and the cricket club moved in, utilising the school for changing rooms. In 1952, Owen White, secretary of both football and cricket teams, re-formed the sports club and the original changing rooms were moved from Glebe Field.

Herriard Cricket Club still use this as a second ground.

HIGHCLIFFE – Wingfields Recreation Ground

Christchurch Borough Council owns Wingfields Recreation Ground. There is one cricket table with seven grass wickets and one artificial strip.

Mudeford Cricket Club use this as a second ground.

Highcliffe Cricket Club use the ground but they only have a Sunday Friendly side.

HOLYBOURNE

HOLYBOURNE CC: Holybourne Cricket Club previously played at a field close to where they play now, but the Second World War intervened and they ceased playing, like most clubs. It took an unusually long time for them to re-form, which they did in 1995, and for a couple of years played at the old Courage/Bass Alton ground. Then the Froyle Estate donated this field to the village, which they rent. The Estate also gave them the shop from the local pick-your-own strawberry field at Cuckoo's Corner to use as the pavilion. The pavilion was extended in 2010 and the clock tower was added in 2016.

HOOK – King George V Playing Field

HOOK & NEWNHAM BASICS CC: This pavilion was built after the previous one, built in 1961, was gutted by fire in September 1971.

Hook & Newnham Cricket Club was formed in 1936 by merging the Water End Cricket Club who played behind the Red Lion pub, and the Hook British Legion Cricket Club who played at Hartletts Park. This ground on Hook Common dates from then. The current club was formed by merging Hook & Newnham Cricket Club with Basics Polhill Cricket Club in 1993.

Hook & Newnham Basics First XI play in the Southern League, with their Second, Third, Fourth and Fifth XIs in the Hampshire League.

HORDLE

HORDLE VILLAGE CC: This fine pavilion, which doubles-up as the village hall, opened in 1999 following a grant from Sport England in 1997.

The village, situated between Lymington and New Milton, includes the hamlets of Tiptoe and Everton. Hordle Village Cricket Club has one senior side in the Hampshire League.

HUNGERFORD – The War Memorial Ground

HUNGERFORD CC: This pavilion opened in 1970. The original prefab pavilion here was destroyed by fire in the 1960s.

Hungerford Cricket Club was formed sometime in the late 1800s, and between the Wars was kept alive mainly through the efforts of the Reverend JF Denning. The present Club re-formed in 1948.

The detailed history from the early part of the nineteenth century is lost, however it is known that a Hungerford team played against the full English professional team in 1852, 1853, and 1854. In July 1852 the England team went to Hungerford straight after a Gentlemen v Players match at Lords. The match was played at Hungerford Park and the England XI were dismissed for 12 runs by the XXII of Hungerford.

HURSLEY – IBM UK Laboratories

IBM HURSLEY CC: This pavilion was opened by the Mayor of Winchester, Alderman CH Bones JP, on 29 April 1966. Five years later the Club obtained a drinks licence, which allowed the sale of beer only! The original clubhouse was the little cottage on the bend in the road between the present club and Hursley House.

IBM moved here in 1958 and the IBM Hursley Cricket Club was founded in 1962. Their first game was away against Strong's of Romsey on 15 May 1962. Strong's brought a barrel of beer along for the occasion. For the first five years IBM played home games at Hursley Park Cricket Club and on Council pitches in Winchester, Eastleigh and Southampton. The first game on the new sports field was on 10 June 1967 versus Castle Cricket Club which ended in a draw.

Located in the grounds of Hursley House, which was built in 1724, it is part of the IBM Laboratories Club which has its own catering staff, so the teas usually receive top marks from visiting teams.

HURSLEY – The Quarters Nursery Ground

The Fielder Pavilion. This was formally opened by the former England cricket captain Rachael Heyhoe-Flint on 20 July 2008. Bill Fielder was a stalwart of the Club for many years and lived in the house overlooking the ground.

It is the second ground at the Quarters and was laid out following the demise of the village football team, as another pitch was needed for their Third and Fourth XIs.

HURSLEY – The Quarters

HURSLEY PARK CC: This pavilion was opened on 27 June 1965 by David Wilkie Cooper, owner of the Hursley Park estate, and was extended in 1974. Hursley Park Cricket Club dates from 1785 and the village team played near the estate entrance where IBM have a second sports field. The Hursley Park estate side used the ground now known as the The Quarters, which was laid out by Sir George Cooper for his son in 1904. The village team moved across the road to the present ground in 1932. During the Second World War American servicemen were billeted here. After the war the ground was restored by Philip Pratt the local butcher, Alex Kew, and George Collins. The existing clubhouse, an old army hut, was brought to the site in 1964 and reconstructed under the guidance of Alan Rodbourne. The old pavilion became the equipment store and was burned down by an arsonist in the early 1980s. The Hursley First XI play in the Southern League, with the Second, Third, Fourth XIs, and Women's Second XI in the Hampshire League. The Women's First XI compete at the top level of women's cricket.

107

HURSTBOURNE PRIORS

HURSTBOURNE PRIORS CC: A letter dated 3 May 1909 from H Plunkett Greene of the Long House proposed the formation of a cricket club to be called Hurstbourne Park Cricket Club, and that Lord Portsmouth would allow the club to use his cricket ground. So the ground existed before 1909, and the club was founded soon after.

Another point of interest is that the Lytch Gate, which is the entrance at the western end of the ground, was built in memory of Beatrice, Countess of Portsmouth in 1937.

The ground is next door to the ancient church of St Andrew the Apostle, which is probably the oldest existing church in the Diocese of Winchester. The setting is stunning. The ground is so pretty that Jocelyn Galsworthy set up her easel here.

HYDE

HYDE CC: Hyde Cricket Club, who run two sides, was formed in 1975 and they had nowhere to play, so they set about making their own ground. After a couple of years changing in a shed, they built this pavilion.

This is another of the New Forest grounds where the wildlife roams free.

Hyde joined the Hampshire League in 1985.

HYTHE & DIBDEN – Ewart Memorial Ground

HYTHE & DIBDEN CC: This pavilion was opened in 1978 when Hythe & Dibden Cricket Club first entered the Southern League. The club as it is known today was formed in 1948 after two clubs amalgamated. The Hythe Club was formed in 1860 and in those days played in a park belonging to their President, Mr J Selmes. The Dibden Purlieu Club originated in Watermans Lane in 1919 and moved to Langdown Lawns in 1934.

After the war they moved to the Power Boat Ground because of bomb damage to their ground in Langdown Lawns. They were then approached by by Hythe & Dibden Sports Club to amalgamate. The newly formed Hythe & Dibden Cricket Club then moved into its new home in Jones Lane. The Ewart Memorial Ground was named after Lieutenant Victor Alexander Ewart RN who commanded a turret on HMS *Queen Mary* at the Battle of Jutland. He was killed in action on 31 May 1916 when the turret exploded. He was 25 years of age.

KINGSCLERE – The Fieldgate Centre

KINGSCLERE CC: The Fieldgate Centre is a community building located close to Watership Down. The centre was built in 1996 at a cost of £1.6 million and is home to many local sports teams and clubs.

Kingsclere Cricket Club was founded in 1774. They moved here from the Holding Ground in George Street.

LANGLEY MANOR – Foxhills

LANGLEY MANOR CC: The pavilion and ground at Foxhills was opened on 23 June 1991 by Ednyfed Hudson-Davies, a former Member of Parliament who later moved to the area and helped set up the New Forest Butterfly Farm. 13 August 1897 is the earliest published record of Langley Manor cricket, when they lost to Mottisfont by 30 runs. Between about 1900 and 1990 the club played at Swinton Field, later known as James's Field, which had three pavilions during their stay, built in 1925, 1954 and finally 1970.

Langley Manor First XI play in the Southern League, with their Second, Third, Fourth and Women's XI in the Hampshire League.

LAVERSTOCK – Sports Club

LAVERSTOCK & FORD CC: In 1942 Laverstock and Ford Sports Club was formed under the patronage of Dr Hill, the owner of Laverstock House. This was based in the old school room situated on the south side of the green, then known as 'The Clump', in the middle of the village. When it first opened there was no money to purchase furniture so the tables were beer barrels and the seating upturned beer crates.

There were additional outdoor activities during the war years including cricket and football. The changing room was an old railway carriage situated at the bottom of the field. Following Dr Hill's death in the early 1950s the club moved to its present location. Funds were raised to build the current club in the 1960s which has been added to and altered over the years.

The Cricket Club was re-formed in time for the 2016 Hampshire League season.

LECKFORD – Baker's Farm

STOCKBRIDGE CC: Leckford Cricket Club was established in 1930 after this 4,000 acre estate was purchased in 1929 by John Spedan Lewis, founder of the John Lewis Partnership. The Club ran the cricket ground until lack of players caused their demise in 2010.

Stockbridge Cricket Club, The Robins, were formed in 2009 and recruited former Leckford players. Stockbridge now have first call at this ground and share it with the Longparish Cricket Club who use it as a second ground for their Third XI.

LIPHOOK & RIPSLEY – Ripsley Park

LIPHOOK & RIPSLEY CC: Liphook & Ripsley moved to this new ground in 1979. The pavilion was re-furbished in 2006.

The Club was first known as Bramshott & Liphook Cricket Club and was founded in the late 1800s. They were known as Liphook Cricket Club by 1973 when they joined the Hampshire League, and played at the Recreation Ground. They became Liphook & Ripsley Cricket Club in 1978 before moving to Ripsley Park, which gets its name from the adjacent Ripley House. Although Liphook is in Hampshire, the ground is in West Sussex. See also, LIPHOOK – Recreation Ground, in Part 2.

Liphook & Ripsley First XI play in the Southern League, with their Second and Third XIs in the Hampshire League.

LISS – The Glebe

LISS CC: This pavilion was built in 1989 and was opened by Club stalwarts Owen and Millie Poulter on 13 April 1991.

Liss Cricket Club was founded in 1880 and played at The Green in West Liss. They have played at the Glebe since 1948 when Mrs Grant, the lady who owned the Old Rectory overlooking the meadow, offered them the field to play in. Following her death in the 1980s her will stated that the club could buy the ground for 50% of its true value. After a fund-raising exercise and grants from various sources the money was raised and Liss Cricket Club had their own ground. Liss currently run two Saturday League teams, a Sunday Friendly side, and a Midweek team who play in the local Ashurst League.

LITTLETON

LITTLETON & WEST HILL CC: An unusual feature of this pavilion is that the changing rooms are in the loft, accessible by the stairs seen on the right-hand side of the building in this photograph.

Littleton Cricket Club was originally formed in 1919. They disbanded and were 'invented' again in 1961 as YMCA (Red Triangle) Club before again becoming Littleton Cricket Club. During the year 2000 the merger with West Hill Cricket Club took place.

West Hill, another long-established Winchester side, had a ground opposite the Royal Hampshire County Hospital, which has now been built upon.

LOCKS HEATH – Locks Heath Sports Club

LOCKS HEATH CC: The Locks Heath Cricket Club crest shows 1894 as a starting date. The Cricket Club is also a section of the Locks Heath Sports and Social Club which is based at the ground.

They have four teams in the Hampshire League and play at three grounds, but this one at Titchfield Common is the main venue.

LONGPARISH

LONGPARISH CC: This pavilion was included in the move when Longparish moved from Top Park to the present ground in 1925, and improvements were made to it in 1967.

Cricket has been played in Longparish since about 1880. Old maps show a cricket ground at Top Park in the north-east corner of the grounds of Middleton House in 1911. The house was bought in 1925 by Captain AS Wills and the cricket club moved down to the village.

LYMINGTON – The Sports Ground

LYMINGTON CC: The pavilion that preceded this one, opened in May 1913 by Viscountess St Cyres of Walhampton, burned down in May 1968.

The first known report of cricket in Lymington appeared in the Salisbury & Winchester Journal of 20 July 1807. They played on Pennington Common until 1836 when they moved to the present ground, then known as Bar Field and later The Cricket Field. Unusually, they continued to play through the Second World War, often against service teams. Work started on a £344,000 upgrade of the pavilion in 2016. Most of the money came from grants from the Football Stadia Improvement Scheme, the ECB, and Lymington Town Council. Lymington First and Second XIs play in the Southern League, with their Third and Fourth XIs in the Hampshire League.

LYMINGTON – Woodside Park

The existing pavilion, photographed in 2006, has been here since around 1982 but in 2014 plans were prepared to upgrade it. The re-vamped pavilion was finished at the end of the 2016 season.

Woodside Park is a 30-acre site originally bequeathed to the people of Lymington by Colonel Henry Douglas Rooke.

Lymington Cricket Club use this ground for their Hampshire League sides.

LYNDHURST – Bolton's Bench

LYNDHURST & ASHURST CC: Cricket was first played at Lyndhurst in the first half of the nineteenth century. The original club was known as the New Forest Cricket Club from about 1840 until around 1900 when they changed their name to Lyndhurst Cricket Club.

In 1989 Lyndhurst merged with Southamptom's Deanery Cricket Club before reverting to Lyndhurst Cricket Club again in 1994. In 2014 a merger with Ashurst Cricket Club took place.

Lying to the east of Lyndhurst, Bolton's Bench is a yew-capped hillock that is one of the village's best known landmarks. The Bench commemorates the 18th century New Forest Master Keeper, the Duke of Bolton. What this Duke of Bolton did to be so immortalised is something of a mystery.

MEDSTEAD – Medstead Green

MEDSTEAD CC: The first pavilion was a wooden building with a thatched roof built some time before 1900. The pavilion was replaced in 1955 by a brick and tile building, which was used by both cricket and football clubs. Around 1990 the pavilion suffered from subsidence and began to split down the middle. It belonged to Medstead Parish Council and they were reluctant to spend money on it so some serious fund-raising took place. This resulted in the pavilion being re-modelled and extended with a first floor being added to give the building that exists today. The extended pavilion was formally opened by Peter May, the former captain of England, on Sunday 14 June 1992. The earliest recorded match here was in 1826.

MICHELMERSH & TIMSBURY – **Mannyngham Way**

MICHELMERSH & TIMSBURY CC: The present pavilion, opened in March 1988, is owned by the Parish Council and leased to Michelmersh & Timsbury Sports Club. The original pavilion on Timsbury Recreation Ground, was built in 1939. Sadly, it was destroyed by fire in March 1986 and with it all photographs showing uninterrupted views of the building.

Michelmersh and Timsbury operated as separate independent cricket clubs until at least as far back as June 1905 when Timsbury Cricket Club played their first game.

MILFORD-ON-SEA – Barnes Lane

MILFORD-ON-SEA CC: This pavilion was built in the 1970s, but was extensively updated and improved around 2007 thanks to a £10,000 grant from the Council.

It is thought that Milford Cricket Club existed in the 1800s and probably played at Newlands Manor, but the present Club was re-born after the Second war around 1946.

Milford-on-Sea Cricket Club now play on this picturesque ground at Barnes Lane Recreation Ground, where they have exclusive rights for the summer season. They are relative newcomers to the Hampshire League, joining in 2002.

MINLEY – Crown & Cushion PH

CROWN TAVERNERS CC: Crown Taverners Cricket Club were formed in the winter of 1969-70. The pavilion was built, and the first game was played on this ground in August 1971. The ground is next to and has close affinity with the Crown & Cushion public house, an olde-worlde pub that dates back to the 16th century which was converted to an ale-house in 1596. Attached to the pub is the stunning Meade Hall, a medieval-style banqueting hall built from timbers reclaimed from wrecks of the Spanish Armada.

MINSTEAD – The Football Green

The Football Green name is a curiosity as it was named thus in 1787 but is now the village cricket pitch. There was another ground in Minstead at Castle Malwood, where the Southern Electricity Board team used to play, but that one is no longer in use.

Cadnam Cricket Club and Paultons Cricket Club both use Minstead as a second ground.

MOTTISFONT – Bengers Lane

MOTTISFONT CC: This pavilion was opened in 1957 by the Club President, Maud Russell, wife of Gilbert Russell a cousin of the Duke of Bedford. The Russells owned and lived in Mottsfont Abbey from 1934 until 1972 despite gifting the house to the National Trust in 1957. Before this the pavilion was the hut that remains to this day by the entrance to the ground, where they have played since 1935.

Mottisfont Cricket Club played a game against the nearby village of Houghton in 1819, which is considered to be their foundation date. The village social club is the Club's headquarters.

As well as playing in the Hampshire League, Mottisfont also play in the Border League, which was inaugurated in 1970 and consists of Clubs who are based within a ten-mile radius of Romsey.

MUDEFORD – Ledbury Road

MUDEFORD CC: The pavilion was built by the players around 2000 with some Council funding on condition that the Council would own the completed building and Mudeford would be the club in residence with first refusal for use, and a reduced rental. It was opened on 26 April 2000 by Hampshire and England spinner Shaun Udal.

Also known as the Seasiders, Mudeford Cricket Club was founded in 1848. The recreation ground at Ledbury Road has been used for cricket since the nineteenth century, probably as far back as the 1860s.

NETLEY – Royal Victoria Country Park

The Gordon Grace Pavilion. Gordon Grace was a remarkable character, a stalwart of the community who owned a gentleman's outfitters in Woolston, still run today by his son. After his playing days were over he founded an evening T20 cricket league, playing four nights of the week on the all weather strip in front of the pavilion that bears his name. Gordon ran the league and umpired every night of the summer season for several years. When he died it was decided to keep the league going and changed its name in his honour. Overlooking Southampton Water, the Royal Victoria Country Park is a 200-acre site. From 1863 to 1966 it was home to the Royal Victoria Hospital. It was acquired by Hampshire County Council in 1969 and the park opened to the public in 1970.

Locks Heath Cricket Club and Sarisbury Athletic Cricket Club both use the cricket pitch here as an out-ground.

NEW MILTON – Fernhill Sports Ground

NEW MILTON CC: This pavilion was opened by Ian Wooldridge, the Daily Mail sports journalist, in 2006. There was a New Milton Cricket Club formed in 1869, but the present Club dates from 1927. They played at both the Memorial Ground ('The Rec') and Ashley Sports Ground until 1961, then exclusively at Ashley until the move to Fernhill in 2003. Fernhill is a 13-acre site with two squares, which in 2012 was accredited with 'Full Gold' status.

New Milton First XI play in the Southern League, with their Second, Third and Fourth XIs in the Hampshire League.

NOMANSLAND – Nomansland Green

This pavilion was opened by Coventry City Football Club manager John Sillett on the 5 August 1987.

A good hit from the pavilion end will end up in Wiltshire as the county boundary is along the road at the other end. The ground must be unique in that it has four trees and a War Memorial inside the boundary!

Nomansland Cricket Club played here from 1926 until 2015 when, due to lack of players, they joined forces with nearby Bramshaw Cricket Club.

OAKLEY – Oakley Park

OAKLEY CC: This pavilion was opened on 8 May 1937 with a match against Sherborne St John.

There is some doubt when Oakley Cricket Club was founded. The club crest shows 1849 but the first game to be played on the present ground was in June 1854. Also, research has shown that cricket was played in a field next to a pub that is now known as the Beach Arms in 1835.

The present Club was founded by Sir John Wallington, although it is said that the original clubhouse on the site was built in 1845 for a club known as Old Muggleton CC.

ODIHAM – King Street

ODIHAM & GREYWELL CC: With financial support from RAF Odiham, the ECB, local businesses and private donations, this new £350,000 pavilion was opened by life-member Sir Tim Rice on 4 August 2013 following a match against Sir Tim's Heartaches Cricket Club. The previous one burned down after a burglary in January 2012, which is sad because it was spared from war damage. The ground is only a short distance from RAF Odiham which was opened on October 18 1937 by General Erhard Milch, Chief of Staff of the Luftwaffe. He was so impressed with what he saw he is reputed to have told Adolf Hitler: 'When we conquer England, Odiham will be my air headquarters', and Hitler ordered his pilots not to bomb the station. The Club's first recorded game was in 1764, which makes it one of the oldest clubs in the world. See also, ODIHAM in Part 2.

OLD ALRESFORD – Upton Park Farm

OLD ALRESFORD CC: In 1982 a disused cricket pavilion belonging to Hampshire County Council was found near a new road in Odiham. It was purchased for the Club and members went to the site and dismantled it. After camping out overnight they took it back to Old Alresford and re-erected it on the cricket ground.

Old Alresford Cricket Club was formed in May 1886. The Rector, Sir FL Currie, was elected President and offered his meadow for the club to play in. After the Great War, the Club was revived on 12 June 1920 and the first game was against Bentworth on 19 June 1920.

OLD BASING – Recreation Ground

OLD BASING CC: The cricket clubhouse on the left is a bar area only and was built in 1986. It was extended and opened by Maria Miller on 22 April 2007. The changing rooms and tea facilities are in the pavilion on the right and has been used by the cricket club since the 1950s. This is the Parish Council building, built in 1951, with the Council offices behind the changing rooms and upstairs. The clock is the 'Millenium Clock'. Old Basing Cricket Club led a nomadic existence from 1815, when they are believed to have started, until 1939. They played at what is now the cemetery adjacent to St Mary's church, a field adjacent to Basing Common, Hackwood Park, and Mapledurwell. In the 20th century Lord Bolton donated a field next to the village brickworks. In the mid-1950s the Holmes family gifted what is now the Recreation Ground to the Parish Council and a permanent home was found for Old Basing Cricket Club.

OTTERBOURNE – Waterworks Ground

OTTERBOURNE CC: Hidden away behind the locked gates of the old waterworks lies this neat little ground. It was the home ground of Southern Water, who used to have a team when Otterbourne Cricket Club played at the top of the hill behind The Cricketers pub, since re-named The Otter. The present Otterbourne Cricket Club grew out of a complex series of mergers which included Antelope, Winchester Castle, Eastleigh, and St Mark's clubs. At the end of 2016 they merged with Colden Common Cricket Club.

Otterbourne play League cricket, but a highlight of their season is the annual North Devon tour which they inherited from Southampton Touring Club after their demise.

OVER WALLOP – Salisbury Lane

OVER WALLOP CC: Over Wallop Cricket Club is a village side that has been going since at least 1884 according to the archives of the local press. The exact date of foundation may go back 50 years before that, according to anecdotal accounts. The Club would appreciate evidence to confirm a more accurate foundation date.

OVERTON – Berrydown Playing Fields

The Ken Hogan Pavilion was officially opened on 19 January 2013.

Ken Hogan was a past Chairman of the Overton Recreation Centre, an organisation that manages 30 acres of sports fields for the 2000 active members involved in sport in the village every month.

Overton Cricket Club Third XI used this ground in 2016, but the improvements being made here may soon result in it becoming the first choice.

OVERTON – Bridge Street Recreation Ground

OVERTON CC: This pavilion was opened by Mrs Miriam Sacher on 17 October 1970. Miriam Sacher (1892-1972) was the daughter of Michael Marks, co-founder of the retail chain Marks & Spencer.

Overton Cricket Club use this as their main ground. They run three teams in the Hampshire League and have another ground at the Berrydown Playing Fields.

OWER – Whitemoor Lane

PAULTONS CC: This pavilion was built in 1962 at a cost of £492. With financial help from the NPFA and the Lords Taverners it was greatly improved in 1965. Further improvements and additions have resulted in the splendid facilities at the ground today. It is thought cricket had been played at Paultons Park before the 18 July 1890 when a match against Downton was reported. The original ground was only a few hundred yards away from Whitemoor Lane. They then moved to a new ground in Paultons Park, to a ground shaped like a horseshoe, where they stayed until 1958. In the 1920s Capt. Lester, an American millionaire, became the tenant of Paultons and he provided the funds to grow the Club. In 1957 it was decided to turn the ground over to farmland, so the Club had to move again. It took three years to prepare the present ground. The Club played away games on Saturdays and worked on the ground on Sundays until it was ready in 1961. Paultons First XI play in the Southern League, with their Second and Third XIs in the Hampshire League.

PARLEY – Parley Sports Club

PARLEY CC: This pavilion was opened on Friday 13 October 1961 by John Arlott and Leo Harrison, the Hampshire wicket-keeper.

Parley Cricket Club was formed around 1945. In 1993 they amalgamated with Springfield Amateurs Cricket Club and with Monty's Cricket Club in 1996. The arrangement to use Dean Park for their senior sides fell through at the end of the 2015 season and this ground in Christchurch Road became their main venue. Kings Park and the Littledown Centre make up the complement of grounds required for their various teams.

Parley First XI play in the Dorset Premier League, but they field four teams in the Hampshire League.

PENNINGTON – Recreation Ground

This pavilion was built in 1965. It was refurbished, and opened by the Director of Leisure Services for the New Forest District Council, Nick Gibbs, on 16 January 1993.

Pennington Cricket Club was formed in 1932 by members of Efford Park private club and Newlands Manor. The Rev LA Hughes bought the ground from Farmer James, and the members prepared the square. The ground was sold to Lymington Borough Council in 1936. Pennington Cricket Club played only in the first year of the Hampshire League.

Sway Cricket Club now use this as a second ground.

PENTON

PENTON CC: Penton Cricket Club was re-formed in 1970, having been wound up in 1964. The club history goes back much further, with score-books back to the 1930s and a match report in the Andover Advertiser in September 1859 of a match between Penton and Andover.

Games in the nineteenth Century were played on a field in Penton Lodge. Some may also have taken place on the Home Farm field just north of the farmhouse adjacent to Newbury Lane. The scores were very low in these games, mainly because the pitches were farm fields which may have had the grass hand-cut for the game. They say the out-field must have been a bit bumpy!

PETERSFIELD – Heath Road

PETERSFIELD CC: The Heath Pavilion was built in the 1970s. In 2015 they raised £100,000, which included a grant of £75,000 from Sports England, to upgrade the pavilion's facilities.

Petersfield Cricket Club was founded in 1751 and have been at the Heath for over 150 years.

This is Petersfield Cricket Club's main ground. They also use a second ground at Penns Place.

PETERSFIELD – Penns Place

Penns Place is the home of Petersfield Rugby Club. The cricket pitch and its tiny pavilion are just a small part of a much larger complex which was opened in 1979.

Petersfield Cricket Club use this as their second ground.

PORTCHESTER – Cams Hill School

PORTCHESTER CC: Portchester Cricket Club was established in 1885. The First and Second XIs play at Cams Hill School. The school was established in 1958 and is one of the few in Hampshire to have its own playing field with a pavilion.

The Third XI play in the beautiful grounds of Portchester Castle where, unfortunately, the changing room is at the back of the public toilets and not suitable for a photograph! However, it takes some beating for scenery. As they say themselves - Castle? Tick. Fort walls? Tick. The sea? Tick. Yachts? Tick . . .

Tea there is taken in the salubrious surroundings of the Castle tea-rooms.

PORTSMOUTH – Drayton Park

BIDBURY CC and RAILWAY TRIANGLE CC: This Portsmouth Council-run park has a decent cricket square. The Drayton Park pavilion has shared use with the Bowls Club.

Both Bidbury Cricket Club and the Railway Triangle Cricket Club use this as their main ground. Portsmouth Rovers Cricket Club, formed by Old Boys from Hilsea College in 1927 and re-formed again in 1947, used it when they were in the Hampshire League between 1973 and 1982.

The Railway Triangle Cricket Club website history page only says for them 'It all started in 1989'.

PORTSMOUTH – Farlington Playing Fields

The Farlington Playing Fields cover a huge area to the north of Portsmouth and has facilities for football and cricket. It also includes the St John's College grounds and pavilion.

Kerala Cricket Club use this as their second ground.

PORTSMOUTH – Langstone Harbour Sports Ground

Railway Triangle Cricket Club use this as their second ground.

PORTSMOUTH – Rugby Camp

KERALA CC and SERVICEMASTER CC: This ground is the home of Portsmouth Rugby Football Club. The cricket pitch is currently used by Kerala Cricket Club, the home of Malayalee cricket in Portsmouth, who use this as their home ground. The Malayalee are an ethnolinguistic group native to the South Indian state of Kerala, hence their name.

Servicemaster Cricket Club use this as their home ground too. Servicemaster Cricket Club was founded in 2009 and is managed by Kevin Riley, the owner of ServiceMaster Clean in Portsmouth.

Portsmouth & Southsea Cricket Club also use the ground for their Third XI.

PORTSMOUTH – St Helen's Field

PORTSMOUTH CC: St Helen's Field is part of Canoe Lake Park which dates from 1886.

The present Portsmouth Cricket Club is the result of a complex set of mergers. In 1937, Portsmouth & Southsea Cricket Club was formed by amalgamating Southsea Cricket Club and Travellers Cricket Club which was formed in 1906. South Hants Cricket Club was formed in 1947. Portsmouth Rovers and Portsmouth & Southsea Cricket Clubs merged in 1983. Finally, in 1989 Portsmouth Cricket Club was formed by amalgamating South Hants Touring Club, Portsmouth & Southsea Cricket Club and Portsmouth Cricket Club Colts.

Portsmouth First XI play in the Southern League, with their Second and Third XIs in the Hampshire League.

PORTSMOUTH – St James' Hospital

PORTSMOUTH & SOUTHSEA CC: Built between 1876 and 1879, St James' Hospital in Milton was the town's lunatic asylum. The grounds were left in a rough state as the plan was to let the patients tend the 75-acre site as part of their treatment.

Portsmouth & Southsea Cricket Club moved to St James' Hospital in the 1980s. The Club was initially formed in 1954 as Enterprise Cricket Club, but in the early 1970s they changed their name to Portsmouth Enterprise Cricket Club. In 1997 another name-change to Southsea Cricket Club was followed by the amalgamation in 2003 of Southsea Cricket Club and Portsmouth Colts to form the present Club.

PORTSMOUTH – St John's College, Farlington

The 40 acres of sports grounds at Farlington known as 'The Fields' caters for cricket, football, rugby, tennis, and netball.

St John's College was founded in Southsea in 1908.

Portsmouth Cricket Club and Purbrook Cricket Club both use the College cricket pitch and pavilion as an out-ground.

PORTSMOUTH – United Services Sports Ground

US PORTSMOUTH CC: There is evidence to suggest that cricket has been played here since 1852. The ground was built on reclaimed land and is owned by the Crown Estate. The first first-class game to be played here was between Australia and a Cambridge University side in August 1882.

Hampshire County Cricket Club played here between 1882 and 2000. It was one of their four home grounds, along with Dean Park in Bournemouth, the County Ground in Southampton, and May's Bounty in Basingstoke. The ground is now the home for United Services Cricket Club and their rugby club.

PURBROOK – Purbrook Heath

PURBROOK CC: The current pavilion here was opened in 2002.

The ground at Purbrook Heath opened in 1953.

Purbrook Cricket Club and Portsdown Cricket Club amalgamated in 1982 to make Purbrook & Portsdown Cricket Club. Purbrook Cricket Club was formed in about 1900. Portsdown Cricket Club was formed from the Christ Church Cricket Club which was developed by the Reverend Frank Worwood in 1951.

The name changed back to Purbrook Cricket Club in 1991.

PYLEWELL PARK – Manor House

PYLEWELL PARK CC: This pavilion is where tea is taken and where the scorers sit. The changing rooms are in the building behind it. A photograph in the pavilion, dated 1905, shows it very much as it is today.

The Club was founded in 1865 and is situated in the beautiful private grounds of Pylewell Park Manor House which is in 100 acres of parkland, steeped in history, that has been owned by the same family since 1874. Positioned on the south coast in the New Forest, the house sits majestically surrounded by traditionally laid out parkland, with unrivalled panoramic views over the Solent.

RAMSDELL – Recreation Ground

RAMSDELL CC: Before this pavilion was built, what is now the groundsman's hut was used as the changing rooms.

Ramsdell Cricket Club have been around for more than 80 years. When the club was formed in 1934 they played at Povey's Farm. After the War the field was no longer available, so, in 1948 they moved to a field on the Ewhurst Road. Soon after that, ten local people put up £20 each to buy this ground for the Parish Council.

The Sunday side is now known as Whiteditch Rams and the winter Indoor League team goes under the name of Ramsdell Renegades.

REDLYNCH – Redlynch Playing Field

REDLYNCH & HALE CC: The Redlynch Sports and Social Club caters for a variety of sports and pastimes. It is where the changing rooms are and where the players go for tea.

Redlynch Cricket Club history dates back to about 1880. In 1991 they merged with Hale Cricket Club to form the present Club.

Redlynch is in Wiltshire and Hale is in Hampshire. The Club is affiliated to both counties as well as the New Forest Club Cricket Association.

RINGWOOD – Carvers Sports Ground

RINGWOOD CC: This pavilion was built around 1958.

Ringwood Cricket Club was once known as 'The Lions of the New Forest' and the original ground, known as the Bickerley, is still a village green that was enlarged in 1990.

Carvers Recreation Ground was originally bought by the town in 1929 from the proceeds of Ringwood's first carnival, and caters for several sports.

ROMSEY – Hunt's Farm

This ground and pavilion was opened on 8 July 1992 by Councillor Ian Carr, Chairman of the Test Valley Borough Council Leisure Committee.

The ground in Timsbury has two cricket tables, with one pavilion that serves both.

Langley Manor, Michelmersh & Timsbury, and Old Tauntonian's & Romsey Cricket Clubs all use Hunt's Farm as an out-ground.

ROMSEY – Sports Centre

OLD TAUNTONIAN'S & ROMSEY CC: Romsey Cricket Club was formed in 1895 although there was a team formed in 1880 by a group of local farmers after a dispute with King's Somborne over eligibility to represent Somborne village. They were originally known as Romsey Farmers Club of Cricketers, and then the Touring Club of Romsey. The present club moved to this ground in 1958.

Old Tauntonians Cricket Club's first full programme was in 1929. They played at Highfield until the School site became part of Southampton University and then had three or four years at Lordshill. The two clubs combined in 1998. OT's & Romsey First XI play in the Southern League, with their Second, Third, Fourth and Fifth XIs in the Hampshire League.

ROPLEY – The Recreation Ground

ROPLEY CC: This pavilion was opened by the former Leicestershire, Hampshire and England cricketer David Gower in November 2005. It was built for Ropley Parish Council and was partly funded by Sport England, East Hampshire District Council, and the Hampshire Playing Fields Association. The initial design was by club stalwart John Sutton, and was completed by Michael Weakley who has been responsible for several cricket pavilions around the county. It is the third pavilion at the Recreation Ground. The first was when the club moved here after the war and was built on the western side of the ground. That was replaced in 1962 by another one, on the east side where the present one is.

Little is known about cricket in Ropley between the wars, but there are accounts of matches played at Ropley House, built around 1750, before the move to the Recreation Ground.

ROTHERWICK – Rotherwick Playing Field

ROTHERWICK ITW CC: This is among the prettiest of the Hampshire pavilions and the one chosen for the front cover of this book.

Rotherwick Cricket Club joined the Hampshire League in 1983 and became Rotherwick BBR Cricket Club in 1998.

The ITW (Illinois Tool Works) Cricket Club joined the League in 1986 and in 2002 the two Clubs merged.

Hook & Newnham Basics Cricket Club use Rotherwick as their second ground.

ROWLEDGE – Recreation Ground

ROWLEDGE CC: This pavilion dates from 1924 and the ground is believed to be one of the oldest cricket grounds in England. It is often referred to as the 'original Oval'.

The first record of Rowledge Cricket Club appears in 1886 with a match against Tilford, but the present Club's official start date is 1887. Until 1914 the club played its home matches at Holt Pound. Since 1914 the club has played at Rowledge Recreation Ground, which has changed little since.

Rowledge First XI play in the Southern League, with their Second and Third XIs in the Hampshire League.

ROWNER – Rowner Green

ROWNER CC: The club was established in 1954 as Bridgemary Cricket Club.

The ground had an artificial wicket until 1964 when a new square was laid and a pavilion built. The club was then re-named Rowner Cricket Club. An oak tree remains within the field of play.

SALISBURY – Skew Bridge, Bemerton - Pitch 1

SOUTH WILTS CC: Now known as the Salisbury and South Wiltshire Sports Club, this £1.2 million pavilion was opened in November 2011 by Sir Michael Parkinson.

This is the Wiltshire County Ground. The first recorded match here was between South Wilts XVIII v All England XI on 26-28 June 1854, which South Wilts won by 3 runs. Perhaps uniquely, South Wilts Cricket Club teams have taken part in the cricket of four counties – Wiltshire, Berkshire, Hampshire, and Dorset.

South Wilts First and Second XIs play in the Southern League, with their Third and Fourth XIs in the Hampshire League.

Their Third and Fourth teams use the second pitch here. See also, the old pavilion in Part 2.

SALISBURY – Skew Bridge, Bemerton - Pitch 2

This pavilion on the second pitch, or the Academy Ground, was built in 1982.

SARISBURY – The Hollow

SARISBURY ATHLETIC CC: The history of Sarisbury Athletic Cricket Club is yet to be written, but they moved to this new ground towards the end of the Twentieth century when they outgrew their original ground on Sarisbury Green.

In 2016 the Club started the season with six Saturday league teams so they required three out-grounds, which included their original home at nearby Sarisbury Green.

Sarisbury Athletic First XI play in the Southern League, with their Second, Third, Fourth, Fifth and Sixth XIs in the Hampshire League.

SARISBURY GREEN

This is a unique ground with, perhaps, a unique rule to protect the passing traffic on the A27. 'Cricket may only be played at Sarisbury Green if the protective netting system is erected prior to each fixture commencing, and is in place for the duration of the fixture. If it is not possible to erect the protective fencing then, regardless of the reason, the fixture must not be played'. Once referred to as 'Saresbury', records of the Hambledon Cricket Club confirm the existence of the Green before 1774.

Locks Heath Cricket Club and Sarisbury Athletic Cricket Club share this ground as an extra venue.

SHEDFIELD – Recreation Ground

Shedfield Cricket Club was founded in 1886, but they disbanded in 2012. The club moved to this ground in the early 1960s, but they never played in the Hampshire League.

The Shedfield Parish Council website proudly states: 'The cricket pitch at Shedfield is regularly used by cricket teams from other parishes who are not as fortunate as we are in Shedfield'.

Fair Oak Cricket Club used Shedfield for their Regional Division side in 2016.

SHERFIELD-ON-LODDON – Goddards Lane

SHERFIELD-ON-LODDON CC: Sherfield-on-Loddon Cricket Club first joined the Hampshire League in 1983 but left before being revived in 1997 after a merger with Fanum Cricket Club, the former Automobile Association's Basingstoke side who were also struggling to carry on at the time. Fanum AA had joined the League in 1987 but became Fanum CC around 1989. They had been playing at Sherborne St John's ground but at the time of the merger were homeless, so they took the Sherfield name. The present Club also play in the Dummer Indoor League as Sherfield Foxes.

Basingstoke & North Hants Cricket Club Fifth XI also share this ground as their home. Their Third and Fourth XIs use the second ground at May's Bounty.

SHREWTON – Recreation Ground

SHREWTON CC: Shrewton Cricket Club is deep into Wiltshire. They joined the Hampshire League in 1998 and have a team in County Division 1 that play here, but they aspire to greater things and in 2016 they are looking to build a new ground to help them achieve this. The new ground would be at Clancy Field in Nett Road, and is planned to have a two-storey cricket pavilion, machinery shed, multi-use games area, and a two lane practice net.

Shrewton also use a second ground at Appleford School, which is adjacent to the Recreation Ground and does not have a pavilion of its own.

SILCHESTER – Silchester Common

SILCHESTER CC: This pavilion is used by the Cricket Club, Calleva Football Club, and Silchester Football Club. The Cricket Club joined the Hampshire League in 2002. 'Home to cricket since the Romans', it says on their website, a reference to the village's ancient history.

Adjacent to the cricket field is the village's only pub, the Calleva Arms, a regular entrant in all the best-beer guides!

SOUTH NEWTON – Recreation Ground

SOUTH NEWTON CC: The pavilion is separate from the South Newton & Wishford Village Hall at the entrance to the ground, where tea is taken.

Located in Wiltshire's beautiful Wylye Valley, South Newton Cricket Club was formed over 100 years ago.

They joined the Hampshire League in 1992, but also play Evening League cricket in the Salisbury & District League.

SOUTHAMPTON – Lordshill Centre

SOUTHAMPTON TRAVELLERS CC: Lordshill Centre, also known as Five Acres, was opened in the 1970s and was for a short time the home ground of Deanery, Old Tauntonians, and Southampton Touring Club, three of Southampton's top sides.

Southampton Travellers were formed in the 1930s as the British Commercial Travellers Association. They amalgamated with the United Kingdom Commercial Travellers Association after the war when the Club was re-formed. After another name-change the Southampton Commercial Travellers have been a member of the Hampshire League since its beginning. They shortened their name to Southampton Travellers Cricket Club in 1980 and are the oldest club in the League playing under the Southampton banner.

SOUTHAMPTON – The Rose Bowl (Nursery)

THE HAMPSHIRE ACADEMY: The Arthur Holt Pavilion. Arthur (1911-1994) played cricket for Hampshire and football for Southampton. He became a coach with Hampshire and, with Reg Haskell, established a successful sports shop in Shirley, Southampton which still trades under their names today. The first game played on the Nursery was 6-9 June 2000 when Hampshire 2nd XI played Sussex 2nds and lost by an innings and 3 runs. A first-class game was also played here on 17-19 April 2013 when Hampshire played Loughborough MCCU, and Hampshire won. It is the home ground for Hampshire 2nd XI and the Hampshire Academy. The Hampshire Academy have a special status within the Hampshire recreational league pyramid. They joined the Southern League in 2002 following Cove Cricket Club resigning their short-lived stay. The Academy enjoys a special status within the League that allows them to register outstanding youth players from other competing sides.

SOUTHAMPTON – Trojans Sports Ground

TROJANS CC: The present 23-acre ground at Stoneham was bought in 1953, and in March 1970 a major extension of the pavilion was opened.

The Trojans Club was established in 1874, the cricket club in 1895. They played at the County Ground in the early days and in 1908 a clubhouse was bought in the centre of Southampton. A move to the Polygon area in 1951 followed, along with sporting activities to Swaythling. The Trojans Club is said to be the largest amateur sports club in Hampshire. There are five main sports played at the Stoneham Lane ground - rugby, hockey, squash, cricket and football, with over a 1000 multi-sports members, and it's all run by volunteers.

Trojans First XI play in the Southern League, with their Second and Third XIs in the Hampshire League.

SOUTHAMPTON – Vosper's Sports Ground

OLD NETLEY & HIGHFIELD CC: This is the old Vosper Thornycroft ground from the days of ship-building in nearby Woolston. The Vosper and Thornycroft companies merged in 1966, and their football and cricket teams shared this ground.

The football team became known as Sholing FC in 2010. The cricket club became Old Netley Cricket Club after briefly being called VT Cricket Club in 2013.

Highfield Cricket Club joined the Hampshire League in 1993 and played at Hardmoor until 2014, when they merged with Old Netley Cricket Club. The combined club made this their new home, ready for the 2015 season.

SPARSHOLT – The Norman Edwards Ground

SPARSHOLT CC: This £8,000 pavilion was built after the club joined the Hampshire League in 1975. It was extended in 1992. Norman Edwards joined Sparsholt Cricket Club in the 1930s and played an active part in the Club until retirement in 1997.

Cricket had been played at various locations in and around the village since the late 1800s. Samuel Bostock gave this ground to Sparsholt Athletic Club in the early 1930s and the present Sparsholt Cricket Club was re-formed in 1935. The first pavilion was a chicken hut, with an attached stable for a horse, that cost just £6.7s.6d. It was replaced by 1949 by another one which was given to them by Mr Bostock.

Sparsholt First XI play in the Southern League, with their Second and Third XIs in the Hampshire League.

ST CROSS

St Cross Symondians Cricket Club was formed in January 1992 with the amalgamation of St Cross Cricket Club, founded in about 1873, and Old Symondian Battery Ramblers Cricket Club.

Old Symondians Cricket Club, formed in 1952, had joined forces with Stanmore Ramblers Cricket Club in the late 1960s, and Olivers Battery Cricket Club, founded 1947, in 1989.

The ground, originally described as 'two meadows', covers two fields of approximately 6 acres each, and are now known as 'the field' and 'the other field'. The Third and Fourth XIs usually play on this, the southern one. St Cross also use the Worthy Down Army Base as an out-ground.

St Cross First and Second XIs play in the Southern League, with their Third, Fourth, Fifth, Sixth and Women's XIs in the Hampshire League.

ST CROSS – Green Jackets Ground

ST CROSS SYMONDIANS CC: The original pavilion from 1886 burned down. It was rebuilt and this one opened in 1970.

The ground has been in use since 1859 when Winchester Garrison played I Zingari. It was first leased to the Rifle Brigade and in 1885 it was leased to the Green Jackets Club. The 'luncheon' pavilion on the south side was built in 1904 and has recently been restored. This ground is where the First and Second XIs play.

The ground is owned by the trustees of the ancient Hospital of St Cross, the medieval foundation which, with its ancient almshouses and chapel, lies just to the north of the field. On 1-2 July 1875, St Cross hosted a first class match here when Hampshire were defeated by Sussex by an innings and 27 runs.

ST MARY BOURNE – Recreation Ground

ST MARY BOURNE CC: St Mary Bourne Cricket Club was founded in 1866 and moved to the Recreation Ground in 1929.

Their Facebook page claims the ground to be the prettiest in Hampshire, if not the World!

STEDHAM – Recreation Ground

This ground has two pavilions but one is used for changing and teas and the other is the score-box.

The Stedham Social Club had plans for a new pavilion here when this photograph was taken in 2008. The controversial £350,000 proposal involved the demolition of the existing clubhouse in The Street and replacing it with four houses. The funds generated by the scheme would finance a new pavilion on the recreation ground.

This West Sussex village is better known as the place where the late media tycoon Kerry Packer caused controversy in the late 1980s when he bought many acres of agricultural land and converted it into a polo centre. It also has a solitary pub, the Hamilton Arms, which doubles-up as a Thai restaurant.

Liphook & Ripsley Cricket Club use this ground as a second venue.

STEEP

STEEP CC: The earliest reference of Steep Cricket Club has been traced to 1892, which is recorded on their crest, when the Rev. EL Puxley and schoolmaster JW Skillington formed the club to keep the villagers out of the adjacent Harrow Inn.

When they restarted in 1948 they played on Steep Common and in fields behind Johnson's Farm. They were based at the Harrow Inn, but resisted being called Harrow Cricket Club to save confusion with the well-known public school in North London. They then bought the freehold of this ground and built the pavilion, which is said to have cost the same as the one built for the MCC at Lords, which was financed by a local man, William Nicholson.

STEEPLE LANGFORD – Langford Recreation Ground

STEEPLE LANGFORD CC: This pavilion was built in 1972 and extended in 1977. The previous pavilion was just a changing room and tea was taken in the Hanging Langford village hall.

Set in Wiltshire's Wylye Valley, the recreation ground was donated to the village by the Andrews family. It is owned by the Parish Council who rent it out to the village cricket, football, and tennis clubs.

Steeple Langford Cricket Club was founded in 1956 and their first game was on 18 May 1957 against Edwards Bros Cricket Club of Salisbury.

STUBBINGTON – Stubbington Recreation Ground

This building overlooks the cricket square, but is the Scout's 'hut' and not the pavilion for the cricket ground, which it sadly lacks. However, plans are afoot for Sarisbury to use it in 2017.

The Stubbington and Lee-on-Solent Cricket Clubs merged in 1947 and became Crofton Cricket Club. Crofton then joined up with Fareham in 1990. See Fareham & Crofton Cricket Club.

At the start of 2016 Sarisbury Athletic Cricket Club had six teams, one in the Southern League and five in the Hampshire League. Stubbington is one of four grounds that they used.

SWANMORE – Recreation Ground, Broad Lane

CricketArchive records show a match between Swanmore Park Cricket Club and Hambledon was played here on 16 August 1880. The current Swanmore Cricket Club only play mid-week and Sunday Friendlies.

Bishops Waltham Cricket Club used Swanmore as a second ground in 2016, but will be using the Holt at Upham in 2017.

SWAY – Jubilee Field

SWAY CC: This photograph shows the pavilion in 2007 when there were plans to replace it. These plans are still in place in 2016, but significant improvements have been made to the facilities in that time.

The earliest mention of a game at Sway was in the 26 July 1873 edition of the Hampshire Advertiser that mentioned a game between Sway CC and Milton CC. That game may have been played on the field in Pitmore Lane which by 1897 had a building marked 'Pavilion' on maps of that time. Not much is known about the Club between the Wars, but it resumed some time after 1945 and played at a ground close to the present one until the 1970s, when they returned to Pitmore Lane.

The present club re-formed in 1992 and moved to the Jubilee Field in 2002 when they joined the Hampshire League.

TADLEY – The Recreational Society

AWE TADLEY CC: The Club started in the Hampshire League in 1973 as AWRE Aldermaston Cricket Club, who were formed in the early 1950s. They became AWRE Tadley Cricket Club then Tadley Cricket Club before settling on AWE Tadley Cricket Club in 1989.

Until 1990 the Recreational Society's groundsman was Eddie Seaward who went on to be Head Groundsman at the All England Lawn Tennis Club at Wimbledon. He received an MBE in 2007 for services to sport.

TICHBORNE – Tichborne Park

TICHBORNE PARK CC: This pavilion has seen some of the World's top players when, in 1965, 1966, 1967 and 1968, Hampshire played a series of matches against the International Cavaliers. The Cavaliers included Colin Cowdrey, Denis Compton, Alan Knott, Godfrey Evans, Derek Underwood, Ted Dexter, Trevor Bailey, Hanif Mohammed, Geoffrey Boycott, Garfield Sobers, Fred Trueman, Jim Laker, Lance Gibbs, Clive Lloyd and Frank Tyson, over the four games.

In 2016 the Club produced a video for the Building a Better Community project, which showed plans for a new pavilion. Tichborne Park Cricket Club was formed by the Tichborne family around 1850.

Tichborne First XI play in the Southern League, with their Second, Third and Women's XIs in the Hampshire League.

TOTTON – Southern Gardens

TOTTON & ELING CC: BAT Cricket Club, formerly Bramtoco Cricket Club, became Totton & Eling Cricket Club in 2007. This new complex was built in 2010 and the pavilion was opened by Simon Jones of Glamorgan, Hampshire and England, on 16 October 2010. See also, the old pavilion in Part 2.

Totton & Eling First XI play in the Southern League, with their Second, Third and Fourth XIs in the Hampshire League.

TWYFORD – Hunter Park

TWYFORD CC: The Pottinger pavilion. This pavilion was opened by the former Liverpool footballer, and Southampton FC manager, Graeme Souness on 3 August 2003. It replaced the small wooden pavilion on the south side of the ground.

The Club was founded in 1892 and was then known as Twyford & Compton Cricket Club. Various fields were used until after the First World War when a permanent ground was obtained in Shawford Park. They played there until 1946, when, thanks to Colonel Curtis the Club moved to Knighton Park where they stayed until 1963 when Hunter Park was opened.

UPHAM – The Holt

FLAMINGO CC and MANSBRIDGE CC: Flamingo Cricket Club was founded at a meeting in the Crown Hotel, Eastleigh on 7 December 1959 from the embers of Eastleigh NALGO CC who were formed in 1934. They played at Bishopstoke Recreation Ground until 1975 when they moved to the Holt. They merged with Eastleigh Corinthians CC in 1977 and Monks Brook CC in 1995. Despite these mergers the Club folded just before the start of the 2016 season. See also, UPHAM – The Holt in Part 2. Mansbridge Cricket Club shared the ground with Flamingo Cricket Club. Mansbridge were formed in 1975 and have had several names of sponsors pre-fixing their name – Hendy Ford, Hendy Lennox, and Denplan, but are now back to the original one. There is also a pub side from nearby Beauworth who play Friendlies here. In 2005 a group of locals from the Brigadier Gerard pub in Horton Heath decided to form a cricket team. That team still thrives today as the Milburys Cricket Club.

UPPER CLATFORD – The Sports Field

UPPER CLATFORD & ANNA VALLEY CC: The plaque on the pavilion says 'This sportsfield was given to the Parish of Upper Clatford by the late Major Godfrey Miller Mundy on 10th January 1948. This pavilion was opened by Mrs P Miller Mundy on August 14th 1954'.

In 1948 Major Mundy of Red Rice donated just over 5 acres of land, situated between Goodworth and Upper Clatford, to the Parish Council for use as a sports and recreational venue.

The ground is shared between the village cricket and football teams.

VERWOOD – Potterne Park

VERWOOD CC: Potterne Park provides the community with 12 acres of grounds for rugby, football, tennis and cricket.

Little is known about the first cricket played in Verwood, but records show a team called the 'Furze Hackers' played on Dewlands Common. It is known that Verwood Cricket Club came together on 6 April 1891 when a meeting was held at the school room in Verwood to form a Committee. The Club's first known match was on 12 September 1891, versus Ringwood. Verwood Ladies played Alderholt Ladies in July 1912, a game Verwood Ladies won by 2 runs. The Club folded around 1960, but was revived in 1963 when Woodland Cricket Club merged with what remained of the Verwood team.

WATERLOOVILLE – Rowlands Avenue Recreation Ground

WATERLOOVILLE CC: Originally this area was part of the Forest of Bere. In 1925 it was bought for recreational purposes and opened in 1927. It is also known as Jubilee Park.

Waterlooville Cricket Club has existed for over 100 years but the current club has it's roots in a 1960s amalgamation with Old Nortonians Cricket Club.

Waterlooville First XI play in the Southern League, with their Second and Third XIs in the Hampshire League.

WELLOW – Wellow Recreation Ground

WELLOW & PLAITFORD CC: This pavilion was given to Wellow Parish Council in 1935, to commemorate the Silver Jubilee of King George V, by Mr JJ Crosfield of Embley Park.

The ground dates from 1888. The Hampshire Advertiser of 7 August 1838 reports 'a game played last Monday against Bramshaw Cricket Club'. That is the earliest known record of a game involving Wellow Cricket Club.

WHERWELL – Playing Fields

WHERWELL CC: The Anna Jenkins Sports Pavilion.

On 20 June 1994 the first sod was turned, but it took six more years before the pavilion was completed in 2000 when it replaced the old pavilion shown in Part 2.

Anna Isabella Jenkins (1868-1959), who donated the field in 1955, was the wife of Colonel Atherton Edward Jenkins who the Village Hall is named after.

Wherwell Playing Fields is a charitable trust which was founded in 1950.

WHITCHURCH – Parsonage Meadow

WHITCHURCH CC: The original pavilion, a tithe barn, was renovated in the early 1970s when Lord Denning, the judge in the Profumo affair, was their President.

Whitchurch Cricket Club has been playing since the late 18th century. They started playing here in 1924.

Parsonage Meadow was also once the home of Whitchurch United Football Club, but they have since moved on.

WHITEPARISH – Memorial Ground

WHITEPARISH CC: The Whiteparish Memorial Centre is located on the Memorial Ground and doubles up as the cricket pavilion which was officially opened on 3 June 2014 by the Duke of Gloucester and the Lord Lieutenant of Wiltshire.

Just one-and-a-half miles inside Wiltshire, Whiteparish Cricket Club came late to the Hampshire League, joining in 2002. The Whiteparish Cricket Club All Star Big Band can often be found entertaining the clients of the pubs in the village. See also, the old pavilion in Part 2.

WICKHAM – Rookesbury Park

WICKHAM CC: The 2009 village design statement observed: 'Wickham Cricket Club is very well established and has its own ground, although there is a great need for a new pavilion'. Well, it took five years and this pavilion was erected in 2014.

John Carpenter-Garnier, who died in 1926, once owned Rookesbury Park. He was a first-class cricketer, playing for the MCC and Oxford University, before becoming a Member of Parliament.

WILTON – Castle Meadows

WILTON CC: Castle Meadows is a ground that only has an an artificial wicket, so progress through the League will be limited if Wilton Cricket Club, who only run one team, stay here. Wilton joined the Hampshire League in 2002.

WINCHESTER – King George V

OAKMOUNT CC: There are two identical pavilions here that serve the two pitches.

This was home to Winchester City Cricket Club when the Hampshire League started in 1973. They were formed in January 1968 at a public meeting which wanted a large city club. A nucleus was formed by combining Eastgate and Castaways Cricket Clubs, but there was no Winchester City Cricket Club by 1974.

Oakmount Cricket Club, who joined the Hampshire League in 2015, use this as their main ground.

Compton & Chandler's Ford Cricket Club and Sparsholt Cricket Club both use KGV as an out-ground.

WINCHESTER – North Walls (River Park Recreation Ground)

RAM CC: There are only two pitches here now. The pavilion used to serve three pitches, but there are only four changing rooms! The Number One pitch at this council-owned ground was once a good quality pitch, where Hyde Ramblers who were Winchester's premier side in the 1960s played.

RAM Cricket Club use this as their main ground. Easton & Martyr Worthy Cricket Club and Sparsholt Cricket Club both use this as a second ground.

St Giles Cricket Club which was founded in 2010 by Mike Warner, grandson of Sir Pelham Warner, and the Willow Tree Cricket Club founded in 1982 in the Willow Tree pub, are also residents. Both play Friendlies or local Evening League cricket.

WINTERBOURNE – The Portway

WINTERBOURNE CC: Winterbourne Cricket Club is believed to have been founded in 1851 and have always played here.

Hampton Park Cricket Club were in the Hampshire League between 2002 and 2011 when they merged with Winterbourne and became Winterbourne & Hampton Park CC for 2012, but one year later the Hampton Park name was dropped.

WINTERSLOW – Barry's Field

WINTERSLOW CC: Also known as 'The Foxes', Winterslow Cricket Club re-located to this new ground and pavilion, which opened in April 2009. See also, the old pavilion in Part 2.

The ground is named after Barry Matthiae, a local grocer and baker and a past President of the Club. Barry died in 1994 and his family donated money to the Parish Council which enabled them to buy the ground and build this splendid pavilion.

WINTON – Winton Oval

C.B.B.E.A. CC: The Winton Oval is part of Winton Recreation Ground that is on land given by the Earl of Malmesbury in 1904. The Earl and Countess opened the 14-acre site in 1906 and by September of that year the cricket ground, which has a running/cycling track around the boundary, was laid out.

C.B.B.E.A. Cricket Club use this as their main ground. Winton Cricket Club now only use this for their Third XI.

WOODGREEN – The Common

WOODGREEN CC: An extension to the pavilion was added in 1996. Woodgreen Cricket Club was founded in 1886.

The village is located on the north-western edge of the New Forest National Park and has a population of less than 600. The Common has been designated a site of special scientific interest.

WORTHY DOWN – Army Base

The original wooden pavilion here was on the eastern side of the ground.

RAPC Worthy Down Cricket Club were members of the Winchester Evening League until about 1998 and played in the Hampshire League between 1992 and 2002, but despite building this new pavilion, not much cricket was played here since then.

The military base was originally built for the Royal Flying Corps In 1918 and became RAF Worthy Down. It then became HMS *Kestrel*, which Lord Haw-Haw claimed had been sunk by the German Navy during the War, before it was handed over to the Royal Army Pay Corps in 1960.

St Cross Symondians Cricket Club used the ground in 2016 for their Fifth and Sixth XIs.

YATELEY – Sean Devereux Park

YATELEY CC: This ground and pavilion opened in 1999.

Yateley Cricket Club was established in 1881. In its formative years they played next to The Cricketers pub at Cricket Hill, before moving to 'The Green' on the Reading Road. See YATELEY, in Part 2.

Yateley play in the Thames Valley League. They also have a women's team in the Hampshire League.

212

PART 2

Other Mainland Grounds

Many of these grounds have been used in the Hampshire League, but most are grounds that have no connection with any League in Hampshire, or are where the club only play Friendlies, are private grounds, or grounds that no longer exist for cricket. Also included are pavilions that have since been destroyed or demolished and have been replaced by newer ones.

For the purposes of this book, all the grounds in the Bournemouth and Christchurch area are given honorary 'Hampshire' status which they enjoyed before the boundary changes in 1974. Some of the other grounds are located outside of Hampshire, but are homes to Clubs that have played in the Hampshire League.

ALDERSHOT – The Army Cricket Ground - Pitch 1

The first pavilion here was constructed in 1887. This pavilion was opened in 1936 by the General Sir Francis Gathorne-Hardy.

Until 2002 it was known as the Officers Club Services Ground. The first recorded match played here was in 1861 between the Knickerbockers and I Zingari.

Nine first-class games have been played here, the first in 1905 and the last in 1964. One of those was The Army against the West Indies in 1933, which ended in a high-scoring draw.

ALDERSHOT – The Army Cricket Ground - Pitch 2

This is the second field at The Army Cricket Ground.

The Surrey side Churt Cricket Club used it for their brief stay in the Hampshire League in 2007 and 2008.

ALDERSHOT GARRISON – Buller Barracks

The scoreboard shows the Home team as RLC (Royal Logistics Corps) when the last game was played here. The Royal Logistics Corps was formed on Monday 5 April 1993, so the last game played here was since then.

Buller Barracks has been sold off by the Army and a huge housing development is taking place. Some historic buildings will be preserved, but it seems unlikely that this will be one of them although it still has the potential to be restored as a cricket ground, or perhaps the village green.

ALDERSHOT GARRISON – The Wavell Ground

This ground is not used for cricket any more. It is said that it dates from the days when the lower ranks weren't allowed to play at the Officers Club Services Ground, so they played here.

ALTON – Anstey Park

The Finnimore Pavilion. This pavilion was opened in September 2013 by Derek Gardner, the Mayor of Alton.

Anstey Park is a 32-acre site and is the largest of the Town Council's parks. Apart from the cricket square, there are four rugby pitches and an enclosed football ground.

Anstey Park was the home for Alton Cricket Club before they moved to the Jubilee Playing Fields. See Part 1.

ALTON – Municipal Ground

Seen here in 2006, the pavilion is all that remains from its cricket days, on a ground that hosted one first-class match. Hampshire played South Africa on 7-8 July 1904.

The earliest reference to cricket in Alton is from 1774, when matches were played on Alton Butts which is now used for visiting circuses and fairs. In 1899, due to the efforts of GJ Poole, headmaster of the local Grammar School, this ground was built. It later became the Courage/Bass Alton Sports Ground and became the home of Alton Town Football Club who have now been re-named Alton Football Club and moved to a new ground at Anstey Park.

BASINGSTOKE – Hackwood Park

The cricket pitch has been unused for some time but a Hampshire XI played an Old Hampshire XI here on 25 June 1991 in a Benefit match for Mark Nicholas.

Set in 260 acres of grounds, Hackwood Park House, which was built in 1680, has been put up for sale in 2016.

BASINGSTOKE – Russell Howard Park

This Basingstoke & Deane Council ground at Russell Howard Park opened in 1967 and offers a wide range of sports facilities including netball courts, three football pitches, a cricket pitch and two bowling greens.

Basingstoke Civil Service Cricket Club and ITW Cricket Club both used this ground in their Hampshire League days.

BASINGSTOKE – Stratton Park

This Basingstoke & Deane Council ground at Stratton Park has three football pitches, a cricket pitch and six tennis courts.

Chase Cricket Club and United Caribbean Cricket Club both used this ground when they were in the Hampshire League.

BEDALES SCHOOL - Pitch 1

This pavilion is at the main cricket pitch at Bedales School, a boarding school at Steep which was established in 1893. There are three schools, Dunannie (ages 3-8), Dunhurst (ages 8-13) and Bedales (ages 13-18).

It is also the home ground for the Gentlemen of Bedales Cricket Club who play Friendlies here. In the 1990s an annual fixture between the teachers of Dunhurst and parents of children at the school was played. This annual 'grudge match' continues to this day. In the early 2000s parents and teachers of the Bedales Schools put aside their differences and formed a combined team to take on local village sides. The Gentlemen of Bedales Cricket Club was born.

BEDALES SCHOOL - Pitch 2

The Sam Banks Pavilion. Completed in June 2013, this 'timber-framed barn' overlooks the astroturf wicket and the Dunhurst sports pitches. It was built by the students and local community and is dedicated to the memory of Old Bedalian Sam Banks, a talented cricketer, who died aged 20 in June 2010.

BENTLEY

The Kingsmill Pavilion.

There is no organised cricket at Bentley any more, but the pitch and facilities are still available for hire.

Odiham & Greywell Cricket Club have used this as a second ground.

BERWICK ST JAMES

The pavilion here was built in 1991.

This Wiltshire ground was used by Shrewton Cricket Club as a second venue in the Hampshire League until 2015.

BIGHTON – McCowen Farm Ground

This pavilion remains but the village cricket team does not. Cricket re-started after the Second war but the team folded in the early 1960s. It was revived about twenty years later and played for another fifteen years before folding again. The field was taken over by the Alresford Rugby Club, which was formed in 1991, but they left to set up a new home at Arlebury Park in 2014.

The ground remains part of the McCowen Farm. Donald McCowen (1908-1998) lived at Bighton Manor and was a rower who competed in the 1932 Los Angeles Olympics after being part of the winning 1932 Cambridge crew in the University Boat Race. He was awarded the DSO and DSC for actions in 1944.

BISHOPSTOKE – Recreation Ground

This ground and pavilion was officially opened on 16 June 1967 with a match between IBM Hursley and the Mayor of Eastleigh's XI.

The original pavilion was replaced, and this £1.4 million one was opened on 21 September 2005 by Councillor Peter Wall, the deputy Mayor of Eastleigh.

The complex is now known as 'The Hub'.

Fair Oak Cricket Club and Flamingo Cricket Club both used this as their main ground when the Hampshire League started in 1973.

BISHOPS WALTHAM – Hoe Road

This was Bishops Waltham Cricket Club's old ground at Hoe Road. It is still used for football and tennis, but not for cricket any more.

The Cricket Club moved to Albany Road in 2001. See Part 1.

BISTERNE

The Bisterne Sports Club pavilion, a wooden building, had to be rebuilt after the war. The thatched roof was retained, but has since been replaced by tiles. During the war the field was ploughed up and it was left to Club members to restore it on its return.

Cricket has finished here since this photograph was taken in 2009.

BODENHAM – Longford Park

Set in the gardens of Longford Castle in Wiltshire, this delightful ground is difficult to access as the house is the family home of the Earl and Countess of Radnor and as such it is not generally open to the public.

It was the home for Longford Park Cricket Club when they were in the Hampshire League between 2002 and 2010.

BORDON – Bordon & Oakhanger Sports Club

'This unique Members Only Club dates back to Colonial days when Britain had an Empire', they say.

The cricket ground and a pavilion were laid out by 1910. The clubhouse was built in 1922 and paid for by serving officers of the garrison. The original cricket pavilion became the groundsman's store. In 1977 the Army vacated the garrison and a decision was taken to hand over the lease to a civilian committee.

The Bordon & Oakhanger Sports Club came in to being in 1980.

BOURNEMOUTH – Dean Park

The Cooper Dean Pavilion. The plaques say 'This Pavilion was built in 1902 by James Edward Cooper Dean for the Bournemouth Cricket and Lawn Tennis Club. Restored in 1990 by Miss Sylvia Bowditch to mark the Cooper Dean family's commitment to cricket and their outstanding contribution to the development of Bournemouth.'

The ground dates from 1869. Hampshire first played here in 1869 and it became one of their four main home grounds, along with Basingstoke, Portsmouth and Southampton, until August 1992.

Bournemouth University, Suttoners, and Parley Cricket Clubs continued to use the ground until 2015, but by 2016 cricket here had ceased.

BOURNEMOUTH – Slades Farm

Slades Farm Open Space sits on land previously known as Talbot Village. Talbot Village was built between 1850-1862 by the Talbot Sisters, Georgina and Mary, to employ and look after the poor of Bournemouth. It consisted of cottages and plots to farm, along with alms houses. A school was built in 1862. It was first proposed to develop the site In January 1973. The playing fields and pavilion were completed by 1978 at a cost of £104,500. By July 1989 Slades Farm boasted facilities that included seven football pitches and three cricket squares.

This ground has been used by Suttoners Cricket Club in the Hampshire League.

BRAISHFIELD

This pavilion at the ground in Dummers Road looks very similar to the previous one that was destroyed by fire.
The legendary Newport Inn is no more, but the cricketers live on. The pub had two teams, one from each bar.
The Newport Inn team came from the Public Bar and the Newport Gents team were 'the toffs' from the Lounge
Bar. The pub has closed but the teams continue to play Sunday Friendlies.

BROCKWOOD – Brockwood Park Farm

This is a private ground used by Brockwood Cricket Club and the White Hunter Cricket Club.

The WHCC was formed in July 1986 to play one match only. By their thirtieth anniversary they had played 342 matches in 2 countries and 15 UK counties, winning 125 and drawing 30. 314 people have played on 73 different pitches against 90 oppositions. They say they remain unbeaten north of Gretna, south of Toulouse, west of Truro, and east of the North Sea . . .

BROWN CANDOVER

This pavilion was opened by Colonel Kenneth Savill on 2 October 1992. It replaced the original hut that was relocated here by the Home Guard in 1947.

Kenneth Edward Savill was born at Three Bridges, Sussex on 8 August 1906 and was educated at Winchester. It was there that he was given the nickname 'Kate'. He died on 29 December 2007 aged 101.

The Candover Valley Club is set in an idyllic location next to St Peter's Church looking out over the cricket pitch. It is also home to the Candover Valley Quilters and the local Cub, Scouts, and Beavers groups.

Cricket came back to Candover in 2003. The John Harkness Cup is played for annually to remember the former President who led the revival.

BURGHCLERE – Burghclere Sports Club

This pavilion was opened on 4 July 1980. It has been extended since this photograph was taken in 2006.

The pavilion before this one was opened on 23 May 1936 by Lt. Col. John Ford Elkington, who had an interesting career. Cashiered very publicly in September 1914, at the very beginning of the First World War, and then rehabilitated in spectacular fashion after winning a Croix de Guerre after he had joined the French Foreign Legion. He was then reinstated to his rank in the British Army. The pavilion was bricked-up and the thatch removed and is now used as a garage.

Burghclere Cricket Club were members of the Hampshire League between 1989 and 2006 and have since disbanded. The cricket pitch is currently being used by Newbury Cricket Club Third XI.

BURITON

This small pavilion is next to the village hall which is used for tea.

Buriton Cricket Club was revived in 2006 and played about twenty matches a year. By 2015 shortage of players meant a reduction of games, but they are still going.

After-match entertainment takes place in the adjacent Five Bells pub.

CHANDLER'S FORD – Hiltingbury Recreation Ground

In 1971 Chandler's Ford Cricket Club moved here from their ground on the corner of Hursley Road and Baddesley Road. They joined the Hampshire League at the beginning in 1973 and stayed until their merger with Compton & Shawford Cricket Club in 1995.

Cricket is no longer played here and the pavilion is now a Community Centre known as The Hilt.

CHANDLER'S FORD – Hursley Road

This is a photograph of the pavilion in Hursley Road from a 1950 painting by Norman Young.

Chandler's Ford Cricket Club was formed in 1912 and the original ground was at Hut Farm in Bournemouth Road where the Hendy Garage used to be.

After the Second World War they moved to Hiltonbury Farm on the south-west corner of Hursley Road and Baddesley Road, which became the housing estate now known as North Millers Dale.

CHICHESTER – Oaklands Park

Bosham Cricket Club has existed since at least 1902. The West Sussex side played at Delling Lane in Bosham until they were told to stop hitting sixes or pack up! So they relocated to Oaklands Park for their Hampshire League games. In 2010 they started to develop a new ground at Delling Close. The first game was played there on 21 June 2015, but as yet, there is no new pavilion. At the end of 2015 they withdrew from the Hampshire League.

Solent Rangers Cricket Club also played here but for 2016 they found a new home at Hayling Park, so the Hampshire connection is now lost.

CHILCOMB – Winchester Castle Ground

Winchester Castle Cricket Club was founded on 23 November 1911 and the first match was against Crawley on 4 May 1912. They joined the Hampshire League in 1982 and stayed until they merged with Antelope Cricket Club in 1995.

This Hampshire County Council Sports Ground is now home to the Winchester Castle Football Club, but there is no cricket here any more.

COMPTON

This was the tea room at Compton Cricket Club which they inherited from nearby Finchdean Cricket Club after they folded. It has now been demolished. The new tea room can be seen behind it as it was being constructed when this picture was taken in 2009. The changing room shown in Part I remains.

COMPTON & SHAWFORD – Memorial Playing Fields

Compton & Shawford Cricket Club moved here after the war. The Shawford Golf Club had closed and this clubhouse was dismantled and re-erected as the new cricket pavilion. See also, Part 1.

CORHAMPTON – Golf Club

A meeting was held at Corhampton House in May 1885 to reorganise the Corhampton Cricket Club on the land of Mr R King Wyndham, who became the club President. A pavilion was built which remained until it was destroyed by fire in the Second World War. The 9-hole golf course was built in 1891, but at weekends cricket ruled and it became a 7-hole course as the pitch was where the first- and second-hole fairways are to this day. Between the Wars, the club was known as Wyndham Cricket Club and cricket finished in 1939.

On 8 September 1991 the Golf Club, by now an 18-hole course, celebrated their Centenary with a cricket match against the Lords Taverners, and reduced the course to 16-holes for the day.

COVE – Grasmere Road

Cove Cricket Club was founded in 1935 and they played at Cove Green. The Grasmere Road ground was completed in 1972 and the clubhouse was opened on 29 September 1972 by Alec Bedser. The first game on 4 May 1974 was against Fleet Cricket Club. On 16 October 1987 the hurricane wrecked the clubhouse. The rebuild was opened by John Bromley (Head of ITV Sport) on 6 May 1988. A later 'improvement' was opened by Robin Smith on 27 March 1999.

Cove Cricket Club now play in the Home Counties Premier League, but had a brief relationship with the Southern League and Hampshire League in 2000 and 2001. It wasn't to their liking and they withdrew.

CRANBORNE – The Mick Loader Memorial Ground

This pavilion was built in 1980. Cranborne Cricket Club (The Cranes) was established in 1857 and until 1884 played on the north side of the Manor. Viscount Cranborne's team then moved to a new site, 'complete with a new tea house', to the east side of the Manor near where the Garden Centre car-park is now for the next 49 years. In 1933 they moved to the present location. In recognition of his contribution, the recreation ground has been renamed the Mick Loader Memorial Ground, a lasting tribute to a fondly missed and great stalwart of the club. Cranborne is in East Dorset, but the Cricket Club had a brief stay in the Hampshire League between 2000 and 2004.

CRAWLEY

Crawley Cricket Club, also known as the Crawley Crows Cricket Club, is a village side who specialise in Friendly cricket.

DOGMERSFIELD – St John-Mildmay Cricket Ground, Chatter Alley

This pavilion was opened on 12 May 1951 and was re-dedicated on 6 August 2001.

The present Dogmersfield Cricket Club was founded in 1947. They now play in the I'Anson League, but were members of the Hampshire League between 1973 and 1992.

Major Sir Henry Paulet St John-Mildmay, 6th Baronet (1853-1916) played cricket for Hampshire in the 1880s, and lived in the Manor House with Lady Mildmay who had the houses she could see from her bedroom window knocked down. Chatter Alley is where the houses were rebuilt to house the re-located estate workers.

DROXFORD

The earliest mention of cricket in Droxford was in 1851, when they 'heavily defeated' Winchester Cricket Club.

This ground features two enormous trees within the boundary.

Droxford Cricket Club now only play Sunday Friendlies.

DURLEY – Wintershill

Located close to the Robin Hood Inn, this old-fashion village ground has only basic facilities.
Durley Cricket Club play Sunday Friendly cricket only.

EASTLEIGH – Fleming Park

This is the pavilion that was destroyed when the Leisure Centre was built. With the new Leisure Centre came Indoor Cricket and in 1976 the Farley's Indoor League started. The Leisure Centre, opened in 1974 by Mary Peters the 1972 Munich Olympics Pentathlon Gold medallist, is to be replaced by a new £25 million facility in 2017.

Fleming Park had three cricket pitches, and was the centre for Eastleigh cricket. Tommy Green, Eastleigh's 50km walk Gold medallist at the 1932 Los Angeles Olympics, was President of the Eastleigh Cricket Association when there was an Eastleigh League. There was a knock-out competition named after him too, the TW Green Cup.

There is no outdoor cricket here any more.

EAST MEON

There is reference to a match in 1796 between a combined East Meon and Petersfield team against a combined Hambledon and Portsmouth side. The village team moved to this ground, then known as Pill Meadow, in 1894.

East Meon Cricket Club is a traditional village team who only play Friendlies.

The Isaak Lions, a team from the nearby Isaak Walton pub, has a Twenty/20 team who also play here. They play 'pub-rules' cricket every Thursday night during the summer, before retiring to the pub.

EAST MEON – Westbury House

The pavilion at the Westbury House cricket ground was converted to a private house and still exists as a summer retreat for the present owner.

The ground, located between the villages of East and West Meon, is opposite Westbury House which itself has been converted, first from a private house to a preparatory school in 1926 and then to a care home in 1982, but that too has now closed.

Westbury House was a magnificent Palladian house that was burned down in 1904 and later rebuilt by Colonel LeRoy Lewis DSO, who used the ground for country house-parties.

EAST TISTED – Rotherfield Park

East Tisted Cricket Club were in the Hampshire League between 1974 and 1976. Rotherfield Park Cricket Club still use this ground for Evening League and Friendly cricket.

The ground is located opposite the estate and Rotherfield Park House, which is a Grade 1 listed building constructed between 1815 and 1821.

EMBLEY PARK – The Hampshire Collegiate School

This ground is for the college use only and there is no league cricket played here. The college also has excellent indoor facilities which are used for winter practice.

The school was first established in 1946. Following various mergers the Hampshire Collegiate School was created in 2006.

Embley Park was the country estate home of Florence Nightingale.

EMSWORTH – Barton's Green Recreation Ground

Barton's Green Recreation Ground is in Leigh Park. The Portsmouth Youth Football League reports 'There are well maintained facilities including limited car parking, toilets, individual changing rooms (you will need to provide your own lock), and showers'.

Emsworth Cricket Club used this as an extra ground between 2011 and 2014.

FAREHAM – Cams Alders Recreation Ground

In November 2015 Fareham Council announced that 'the sports facilities at this recreation ground were tired and dated so the Council is proposing to provide a new modern clubhouse and community facility'. Park Lane, Corinthians, Portsmouth Corinthians, and Sexton Gould Cricket Clubs all used this ground in the past, but no Hampshire League side was using it in 2016.

FARLEIGH WALLOP

The pavilion is at what was the private ground of Lord Portsmouth but since 2014 has been looked after by his son, Viscount Lymington.

Set in over 5,000 acres, the Farleigh Estate has its own Social Club which was founded in 1934 for the workers on the estate. The current Social Club was built in 1985 and it is where the cricketers retire to after a game.

FARNBOROUGH – King George V Playing Fields, Knellwood Park

This was one of the grounds that Farnborough Cricket Club used during their Hampshire League days between 1973 and 1986. It has a grass square and is available for hire. It has no resident Club but the ground wasn't booked at all for cricket in 2016.

Farnborough Cricket club was formed in 1927 when they were known as Lynchford Road Cricket Club.

FARNBOROUGH – 6th Form College

This cricket ground was used by the Farnborough Old Boys Cricket Club during their short stay in the Hampshire League between 2006 and 2008.

The College was originally founded as the Farnborough Grammar School in September 1936. It has been a Sixth Form College since 1992.

FLEET – Calthorpe Park

Calthorpe Park is one of the largest areas of community land in Fleet and is home to the town Football and Cricket teams as well as the Scouts, Sea Scouts, and the Council tennis courts.

Fleet Cricket Club's first recorded game was in 1893 versus The Royal Engineers, which they won. This ground has been their home since 1905. Fleet Cricket Club play in the Thames Valley League.

FLEET – Cody Sports & Social Club

The changing rooms are in the Sports Club. There has been a sports and social club at the Pyestock Sports Ground in Fleet since 1948.

In 2002 it was re-named the Cody Sports & Social Club, named after Samuel Franklin Cody the Wild West showman and an early pioneer of manned flight. In 2010 membership was opened up to the local community.

There are two cricket squares here. Cody Cricket Club have now disbanded, but Fleet Cricket Club use this as an out-ground.

FORDINGBRIDGE – Fordingbridge Centre

The pavilion on the right in this picture was used by Fordingbridge Cricket Club.

Fordingbridge Turks Football Club was founded in 1868 and play here, but Fordingbridge Cricket Club, who played in the Hampshire League between 1981 and 2002, is no more.

FOUR MARKS – Recreation Ground

This pavilion opened in 2000 and is now used by various sports, but not cricket.

Four Marks Cricket Club was founded in 1965. Their Hampshire League membership lasted from 1987 to 2013, when sadly they folded.

GOSPORT – Gosport Park

Gosport Park was opened on 17 June 1891 and it cost about £3,000.

There is no cricket here any more. It is now home to the Gosport & Fareham Rugby Football Club.

Alverstoke Cricket Club was founded in 1957 and they played here in the Hampshire League between 1973 and 1988.

GRAYSHOTT – The Sportsfield

This pavilion was built in 1952.

Grayshott Cricket Club, who currently play in the I'Anson League, was founded in 1896. They played in the Hampshire League between 2007 and 2010. The club moved to this ground soon after the First World War.

A second ground at Broxhead Common, the former home of Lindford Cricket Club, was taken over by Grayshott in 2016.

The I'Anson League was founded on 23 January 1901 at a meeting in the Fox and Pelican pub in Grayshott that was chaired by Edward Blakeway I'Anson, who donated a cup. It has member clubs from Hampshire, Surrey and Sussex and is believed to be the oldest continuously-operating village cricket league in England, possibly the World.

HAMBLEDON – Broadhalfpenny Down

This splendid pavilion was opened on 22 June 1999. It is on the site of the original Hambledon Club which was founded in about 1750. By 1760 the Club and the adjacent Bat & Ball pub had become the centre of the cricket world. The last match played in that era was in 1792 and the field lay fallow for 116 years.

A match between a Hambledon XII, which included CB Fry, and an All England XII captained by Gilbert Jessop was played from 10 to 12 September 1908.

Winchester College bought the ground in 1924 but it was 1936 before regular cricket resumed. It is now the home of the Broadhalfpenny Brigands Cricket Club which was established in 1958 by officers of the Royal Navy so that cricket could once more be played on the historic Broadhalfpenny Down.

HANNINGTON – Michael's Field

The plaque on the pavilion tells the story of this ground.

MICHAEL'S FIELD

This playing field
was presented to Hannington by

Bishop Henry Mosley
in memory of his son

Capt. Michael Henry Mosley M.C.
- - The Rifle Brigade -

Killed in action at El Alamein on 2 November 1942.

affiliated to the National Playing Fields Association

HAWKLEY – Upper Green

This was the pavilion in 2006. Since then they have upgraded it by adding new changing rooms, showers, kitchen, bar and veranda, which helped them win the Hampshire Cricket League award for the 'most improved ground' in 2011.

Hawkley Cricket Club was founded in 1890 and have had two spells in the Hampshire League, between 1973 and 1980, and 2010 and 2015.

HAWLEY – Blackwater & Hawley Leisure Centre

The first pavilion here was opened on 28 December 1897 and cost £456.8s.6d.

Between 1912 and 1978 the club was known as Hawley & Bridge Memorial Cricket Club. When this centre was opened in 1978 it reverted to Hawley Cricket Club.

Hawley is on the border of Hampshire, Surrey and Berkshire, but they play in the Berkshire League.

HEDGE END – Norman Rodaway Playing Fields

The Norman Rodaway Pavilion was opened on 16 March 1991 by Southampton and England footballer Mick Channon.

Hedge End Cricket Club used it in the Hampshire League between 1999 and 2005 but cricket has not been played here since about 2007.

HIGHCLERE CASTLE

This is Lord Carnarvon's private ground. In 2006 when this photograph was taken, the fixture card shows eleven Friendly matches.

The 5,000-acre estate with a park designed by Capability Brown has its own cricket club. Founded in 1891 as Highclere Castle Cricket Club it was re-named Highclere Cricket Club in 1929, but during World War 2 the pitch at White Oak was ploughed up. It was re-laid in 1949 and play began again in 1951.

Highclere & District Cricket Club joined the Hampshire League in the beginning, but left in 1976.

The 'Downton Abbey Cricket Club' played against the village here in the eighth episode of Series 3 of this television period drama.

HINDHEAD – Playing Field

Sir Arthur Conan Doyle had his own team at Undershaw in Hindhead. When his team disbanded players from Hindhead and Grayshott formed their own sides.

Although in Surrey, but close to the borders of Hampshire and Sussex, Hindhead Cricket Club were established in 1910 and had several homes before moving here in the mid-1930s. They had a brief membership of the Hampshire League between 1973 and 1976 but now play in the l'Anson League.

HINTON ADMIRAL – Old Vicarage Hotel

The steps to the players' balcony at Northlands Road were preserved here when Hampshire CCC moved to the Rose Bowl.

Commoners Cricket Club played their Hampshire League home games here between 2005 and 2007 and Friendly cricket continued thereafter.

The hotel was refurbished in 2014, cricket finished, and the steps were burned!

HINTON AMPNER

There has been no cricket here since the 1970s, but in 2016 the pavilion was restored to the original concrete base from which it was taken to become the gamekeeper's shed in another part of the estate. The long-term hope is that the cricket pitch can also be restored and that cricket will once again be played at the ground, possibly involving neighbouring village Kilmeston.

Better known for its garden and elegant country house set in 12 acres of grounds, this used to be the home of Hinton Ampner Cricket Club.

KINGSLEY – Kingsley United Sports Club

Established in the 1960s Kingsley United Sports Club provides facilities to the community throughout Bordon. Kingsley Cricket Club play in the l'Anson League.

KING'S SOMBORNE – Recreation Ground

The pavilion doubles up as the Village Hall and is used for a variety of activities.

King's Somborne Cricket Club was founded in the late nineteenth century. They only play Friendlies.

KINGS WORTHY – Eversley Park

Worthies Sports Cricket Club was founded in 1952 as part of the Worthies Sports & Social Club which was then known as Worthies Sports & Athletic Club. A few games were played at Worthy Down until a cricket square was prepared and ready to use in August 1972 at Eversley Park.

Eversley Park is owned and maintained by Kings Worthy Parish Council and is named after Lord Eversley, a cabinet minister who lived at Abbotsworthy House.

The Club played in the Hampshire League between 1973 and 1993. By 2016 the cricket nets were the last sign that the game was played here.

KNOWLE – The Green

This is Hampshire's newest village and is built around 'The Green'.

Knowle Village Cricket Club was founded in 2009. They joined the Hampshire League the following year but in 2016 local politics forced the cricket club to re-locate and they set up a new home at Botley.

LANDFORD

The Sports Pavilion at Landford Recreation Ground has had a facelift. It now boasts a new kitchen area and the changing rooms have had new purpose-made benches installed. This work was made possible by a grant from South Wiltshire Area Board and donations from users and residents. The Pavilion refurbishment is part of a larger on-going project to improve the facilities at the ground to encourage greater participation in outdoor activities by residents of all ages.

This ground is just over the border in Wiltshire and has been used as second ground for Bramshaw Cricket Club.

LAVERSTOKE – Laverstoke Park

Overton Rugby Club, the current tenant's address is 'The Old Cricket Ground, Odd Ball Lane, Laverstoke', which gives away the history of the ground at which Hampshire Second XI played Kent in 1967.

The pavilion is all that remains of the cricket ground and unfortunately, the tent-like 'extension' is a permanent fixture and spoils the view of the traditional thatched building behind it.

LINDFORD

Grayshott Cricket Club inherited this ground at Broxhead Common in 2016. It was the former home of Lindford Cricket Club who also played in the I'Anson League but sadly folded in 2015 due to lack of players.

Lindford is a village of approximately 2,700 inhabitants about seven miles east of Alton. It only became a distinct Parish with its own Parish Council in 1982, but it is an old settlement with a long history. From 1929 to 1982 it was part of Whitehill, and for centuries before that it was part of Headley. Broxhead Common is a Nature Reserve and is particularly spectacular in late summer when the heather is out.

LINKENHOLT

The earliest records show that cricket was played here in 1914. Linkenholt Cricket Club re-formed in 1946. They played in the Hampshire League from 1978 to 2009 and in 2016 they were still playing Sunday Friendlies.

The ground was sold in May 2009 to Swedish businessman Stefan Persson. Included in the estimated £25 million deal were an Edwardian-style manor house, 1,500 acres of farmland, a 425-acre wood, and 21 cottages which are leased to the villagers.

LIPHOOK – The Recreation Ground

Liphook & Ripsley Cricket Club used this ground before moving to Ripsley Park. They continued to use this as a second ground till 2004 when they moved to Stedham.

Cricket is no longer played here but the pavilion remains in use for the local Football Club.

LONGSTOCK

Cricket is no longer played here, but the field and pavilion remain.

The resident bull allowed this photograph to be taken in July 2016, before he and his friends saw the photographer off the premises.

The original cricket field was just above the vicarage in Church Road. In 1916 they moved to this field, known then as 'Mr Chandler's Field'. The pavilion was originally the Parish Room, used as the Village Hall then, and was situated at the entrance to the vicarage. It was enlarged considerably for the Cricket Club when it was moved.

LORD WANDSWORTH COLLEGE - Long Sutton Playing Fields

Lord Wandsworth College has excellent cricket facilities and county standard pitches.

The college has ten grass nets and four grass pitches at the senior school. The Junior School has two astroturf pitches and two astroturf nets. The College has long been recognised for its girls' cricket.

Odiham & Greywell Cricket Club used this ground when they returned to the Hampshire League in 2009.

LOWER FROYLE

This is the pavilion that was built in 1956 by local builder Dick Goodyear as changing rooms for the then flourishing cricket team. It was taken over later on by the Froyle football team but by the late 1970s it was falling to bits.

The present Village Hall on the recreation ground would make a fine pavilion, but cricket is no longer played here.

LYNDHURST - Swan Green

This pavilion was renovated in the early 1990s.

Swan Green is a unique and picturesque ground that has been here since 1883 when Lord Londesborough, a Tory MP and friend of WG Grace, started a club for his family and their school-friends and the Swan Green Cricket Club was established.

In 2013 the Leicestershire, Hampshire, and England bowler Alan Mullally joined the Club with the intention of raising its profile and scoring his first century! Unfortunately at the AGM on 21 November 2013 it was agreed to dissolve the Swan Green Cricket Club.

MEONSTOKE – Recreation Ground

The Meon Hall. This Hall was designed and built by the people of Meonstoke, Exton, and Corhampton in 1979-81. It was opened by HRH The Duchess of Kent on 22 April 1982.

There is no League cricket played on the artificial wicket here, but some games are still played and the basic scoreboard on the wall suggests recent use.

MICHELDEVER

Micheldever Cricket Club played in the Winchester Evening League at this ground which was situated behind the Half Moon & Spread Eagle pub, a beautiful old drovers' inn dating back to 1703.

The Club was asked to make improvements to the pavilion to continue their tenancy after it fell into disrepair. They were unable to agree to the terms, so departed to a new pasture, and another ground was lost.

MIDDLE WALLOP – Army Aviation Centre Ground

Situated off the air-base, the cricket field is part of the Army Aviation Centre sports facility.

RAF Middle Wallop opened in 1940. In 1957 the Army aviation became independent of the RAF and transferred to the new Army Air Corps. It changed its name to the Army Aviation Centre in 2009.

MIDHURST – The Ruins Ground, Cowdray Park

This picturesque West Sussex ground is set between the historic Cowdray Ruins and the Cowdray Polo fields. Midhurst Cricket Club was founded in 1806. Their membership of the Hampshire League ceased in 2014 but they still play here and have a thriving Junior age-group set-up.

Midhurst also use Rogate and Easebourne as out-grounds.

NEW MILTON – Ashley Sports Ground

Ashley Sports Ground is now the home of the New Milton & District Rugby Club who lease the first floor of the pavilion as a Social Club. Cricket is not played here any more.

New Milton Cricket Club and Rydal Cricket Club used this ground before moving to their own grounds in the early 1980s.

NORTH BADDESLEY

This ground on the corner of Castle Lane and Botley Road is no longer used for cricket.

North Baddesley Cricket Club played here until 1998 when they moved to the adjacent field.

North Baddesley amalgamated with Knightwood Park Cricket Club, who had a brief one-year association with the Hampshire League in 2004, and moved to Knightwood Leisure Centre in 2005 before merging with Ampfield Cricket Club in 2014.

NORTHINGTON – New House Farm

This is a private ground that has not been used since 1997, but the pavilion remains.

Sundowners Cricket Club used to play here. A condition of playing for them was that no-one left the ground before sundown! The Fixture Card for their last season in 1997 shows eight fixtures.

CricketArchive shows a game played between FOG Lloyd's XI and The Forty Club on 26 July 1953. When Windward Cricket Club from Barbados toured in 1995 they were entertained here by the Cricket Society.

ODIHAM – King Street

Odiham & Greywell Cricket Club now have a new pavilion since this one was burned down after a burglary in 2012. See Part 1.

OWSLEBURY

In 1906 the owner of Longwood gave this ground to the village and it took two years to make it playable. Owslebury Cricket Club celebrated 100 years at this ground in 2008.

Cricket in Owslebury dates from the 1830's. A newspaper cutting of 1840 states: 'The Cricket Club played courtesy of landowners at Marwell or Longwood'. Lord Tennyson is said to have played for the village while a guest at Marwell.

Owslebury had two goes at Hampshire League cricket, but now only play in the Winchester Evening League, and Friendlies.

PORTCHESTER – Wicor Recreation Ground

Fields in Trust say 'A modern pavilion that provides good changing/washing facilities' so it has changed since this photograph was taken in 2004, but cricket is not played here any more.

Situated on the edge of a small network of tidal estuaries known as Fareham Lakes, to the west of Portsmouth Harbour, Portchester Cricket Club used this ground before moving to Cams Alders School and the Portchester Castle ground.

PORTON DOWN

A request to enter Porton was refused, so this photograph was supplied by their Facilities Management Department.

Wiltshire's Porton Camp Cricket Club played in the Hampshire League between 1977 and 2004.

Soon after they left the Hampshire League in 2004, they made a new pavilion. Cricket is still played here, but you still can't take cameras in!

PORTSMOUTH – Eastney Sports Ground

Cockleshell Community Sports Club is a joint venture community partnership between Meon Milton Youth Football Club and Mayville High School to manage and maintain the facilities at Eastney Sports Ground that was formerly the playing field of the Royal Marines barracks.

This 20 acres of green space tucked behind houses on Southsea seafront adjacent to the Royal Marines Museum has been made available to a number of organisations in the city.

Duck Cricket Club played their Hampshire League games here between 2006 and 2009.

PORTSMOUTH – Portsmouth Grammar School, Hilsea

The Fawcett Pavilion. Derek and Frances Fawcett opened this pavilion on 3 October 1992.

Hilsea Playing Fields are located approximately four miles away from the main school campus and provide the facilities for the majority of the outdoor sports programme. The 17.5-acre playing field is home to four rugby pitches, an astroturf pitch for hockey, five netball courts, seven tennis courts and two cricket squares.

Old Portmuthians Cricket Club played here in the Hampshire League between 1973 and 1977 and although the School originated in 1732, the Old Boys Cricket Club was formed around 1948.

PRESTON CANDOVER

The Preston Candover Recreation Ground is a four-acre field located on the south-eastern edge of the village. It was bequeathed to the village and is run by the Preston Candover Recreation Association,

Cricket is not played at this ground any more but a local estate agent recently advertised that 'Lower Farm in Preston Candover is a house dating from the 18th century, is built of colour-washed brick, and looks out across an immaculately mown cricket pitch'. The £2.5 million asking price neglected to say if a pavilion was part of the deal.

ROCKBOURNE – Recreation Ground

The pavilion here dates from about 1965, but the ground was first used in 1922. It was used for New Forest League cricket by the Hyde and Rockbourne Cricket Club.

Ellingham, and Centurions Cricket Club, have used it as a home ground in the Hampshire League.

ROGATE – North Street

This ground is in West Sussex between Petersfield and Midhurst and is the home of Rogate Wayfarers Cricket Club.

Midhurst Cricket Club used it as a second ground when they were in the Hampshire League.

ROMSEY – Stanbridge Earls School

The school, set in a 54-acre site, closed in 2014. The main building is a Tudor mansion and facilities at the school included an indoor swimming pool, tennis courts and this cricket pitch. It was sold for £10 million and the plan is to build a retirement village of 100 homes on the site, with the main building being retained. Perhaps they will find a use for this neat little pavilion.

ROWLANDS CASTLE

This photograph was taken in 2009 and by 2013 the Council started a modernisation programme to upgrade the facilities.

DACD Cricket Club is a friendly veterans' cricket club, based in Rowlands Castle. 'Always looking for new teams to play, who play just for fun', says their Facebook page.

Rowlands Castle Cricket Club used to play here, but they re-named themselves Stansted Park Cricket Club and moved into the next county. They, too, specialise in Friendly cricket.

SALISBURY – Bishopdown Farm

The plaque in the pavilion says: 'This Community Centre was provided by DJ Pearce Esq. In 1997'.

Both Bishopdown Farm and Hampton Park Cricket Clubs used this Wiltshire ground in their Hampshire League days. Hampton Park joined up with Winterbourne Cricket Club in 2012.

SALISBURY – Harnham Recreation Ground

Harnham Recreation Ground, in the south west of Salisbury on the River Nadder, affords stunning views of Salisbury Cathedral.

Idlers Cricket Club used this as their home ground in the Hampshire League but moved to Leckford in 2013.

South Wilts Cricket Club used it as an extra ground. Wilton Cricket Club moved from here to Castle Meadows in 2016.

SALISBURY – Hudson's Field

Hudson's Field is a large open space to the north of Salisbury in the shadow of the remains of Old Sarum. The field is used for rugby and football and has two squares for cricket.

Milford, and Salisbury Wanderers Cricket Clubs used it when they played in the Hampshire League.

SALISBURY – Skew Bridge, Bemerton - Pitch 1

Home of South Wilts Cricket Club, this is the old changing room block, which was built in the 1960s. It was knocked down after Sir Michael Parkinson opened the splendid new £1.2 million pavilion in November 2011. See Part 1.

SELBORNE

This pavilion is still there and used as a local amenity. A concrete strip in the middle of the field looks like it could host a game if a suitable piece of coconut-matting was provided. Also, in 2016 the stumps and pads were still in one of the cupboards.

Selborne Cricket Club folded in the late 1990s after the closure of Maltby's Engineering works which was situated in the middle of the village and is now a small housing estate. The main participants of the cricket club were the workers at Maltby's who, having lost their jobs, couldn't afford to remain in the village and moved away, thus significantly decreasing the Club's membership and eventually causing its demise.

SHEDFIELD – New Place

New Place is a hotel and conference centre set in 32 acres of parkland.

IBM South Hants Cricket Club used this ground for their Hampshire League matches for a few years, but there are no 'facilities' at the pavilion here so they re-located to Botley. However, IBM still use this for their Sunday Friendlies.

SHERFIELD ENGLISH – Steplake Lane

The shell of this new pavilion was erected in 2016, with a completion date anticipated in 2017.

The ground was a Millennium project which started in 2000 and has facilities for bowls, cricket, croquet, football, rounders, and tennis.

In January 2012 plans were submitted for a new £300,000 pavilion to be ready by 2013, but sufficient funds weren't realised. This new venture has so far cost £50,000, with more fund-raising required to fit it out. It is hoped that the village cricket team will be revived.

The annual 'Village v Manor' match has kept the cricket pitch active and neighbouring Whiteparish Cricket Club used the ground when they were building their new pavilion in 2013.

SOBERTON HEATH – Recreation Ground

The pavilion on the recreation ground was erected in 1951 to commemorate the Festival of Britain.

The history of cricket in Soberton is sketchy and hard to pin down, but it is known that games between the village and neighbours Newtown continued up to the 1970s. There seems to have been a Club between 1932 and 1965 and the Reverend Cardale tried unsuccessfully to revive cricket in the village in 1972. Today the old pavilion remains with a more modern one alongside which is the Guides headquarters. The field has been taken over for football.

SOUTHAMPTON – AC Delco Ground

This ground is now known as Stoneham Park, but there is no cricket any more and it is soon to become a housing estate.

Bitterne Cricket Club used it in their Hampshire League days.

SOUTHAMPTON – Bitterne Park Recreation Ground

Bitterne Park Recreation Ground, specifically the football pitches immediately behind the school, have a long history. There are references to it in council minutes going back to 1934 and the houses that back onto this area in River View Road also date from that time.

There is no cricket here any more, but it is where organised cricket started for the author. Bitterne Park Junior School played on a coconut-matting covered concrete strip in the middle of the recreation ground, between the two football pitches.

SOUTHAMPTON – County Ground, Northlands Road

The ground was opened by the Countess of Northesk on 9 May 1885 and was the County's headquarters until it was demolished in 2000-2001 after Hampshire CCC moved to the Rose Bowl.

The original pavilion here was built by 1887 and by 1895 two smaller buildings were built, one either side of it, with the one on the left becoming the Home dressing room. The Away dressing room was downstairs in the main pavilion, beneath the bar.

The twentieth century saw it modified and extended upwards, with the main pavilion being replicated to form the Ladies pavilion. The two were joined together in 1964 after the 'hutch', as the small building between them was known, had been demolished.

SOUTHAMPTON – Green Park

There is a lot of green space in Millbrook. As well as Green Park there is Mansel Park, Test Park, Millbrook Recreation Ground, and the now-abandoned Studland Road ground where representative games were once held on a very good quality pitch. Most of these grounds were venues for the Southampton Evening Cricket League but, apart from Millbrook Rec, there is no cricket here any more.

SOUTHAMPTON – Hardmoor Playing Field

This ground next to the very noisy M27 motorway was originally made for Taunton's School in the late 1950s. Highfield Cricket Club made it their home before teaming up with Old Netley Cricket Club in 2014, when they moved to the Vosper's ground in Sholing. See Part 1.

SOUTHAMPTON – Hoglands Park

This is one of five central parks in Southampton that were established between 1854 and 1866.

This photograph, taken from Pitch 1 in 2008, shows the pavilion on the right. The toilet block, on the left, also housed the ground equipment, with the scorers and scoreboards stationed on the roof. Situated in the centre of the city behind the High Street, there used to be three pitches here and the pavilion served all three in one large room. The 'postage-stamp' Pitch 3 is now no longer in use.

The Southampton Evening Cricket League was formed in 1931 and there was also a Parks League that played on Saturday. This was where many of the fixtures were played. The main pitch was used for the Final of the AJ Day Shield, a tournament that attracted large crowds in the 1950s.

SOUTHAMPTON – Montefiore Ground

This was the Southampton University ground in Wessex Lane, Swaythling. Around 1925 Florence Montefiore, wife of Claude Montefiore, purchased a piece of land opposite South Stoneham House and gave it to the House for a playing field. Claude paid for a pavilion to be constructed on the land.

The wicket here was second in quality only to the County Ground. There were two squares, and in the days before League cricket the University, Deanery, Southampton Wednesday, and Southampton Touring Club were among the best sides in town, and they all played here.

The Halls of Residence, that are now where the ground and pavilion used to be, opened in 1966. The photograph shows the removal of the turf. There's a nice lawn out there somewhere!

SOUTHAMPTON – Riverside Park

The pavilion here was damaged by fire in July 2005 and was rebuilt by March 2007 at a cost of £750,000.

The two pitches here are used mainly for Southampton Evening League games, but Krakatoa, Riverside, St Georges Guild, and St Mark's Cricket Clubs are among the clubs who played Hampshire League cricket here.

SOUTHAMPTON – Rose Bowl

The Rod Bransgrove Pavilion. The pavilion was so named on 15 September 2015. Rod became Chairman of Hampshire County Cricket Club in 2000 and has seen the ground develop from a field in West End to an internationally-renowned Test Match ground. The ground and pavilion were designed by Sir Michel Hopkins. Surprisingly, it has never been 'officially' opened. Following the move from Northlands Road at the end of the 2000 season this became the new County Ground and the first match here was against Surrey in the Benson and Hedges Cup on 4 May 2001, after the game scheduled on the 2 May against Essex was rained off. The first first-class game was against Worcestershire on 9-11 May 2001, which Hampshire won by 124 runs. It became a Test Match Ground on 16-20 June 2011 when England played a drawn game against Sri Lanka. In 2012 Hampshire Cricket raised money by selling the naming rights for the ground and for now it is known as the Ageas Bowl.

SOUTHAMPTON – Sports Centre

The changing room block at the bottom of the hill serves all pitches.

There used to be five cricket pitches here but the 'postage-stamp' pitches 3 and 4 are no longer in use. Number 1 was a quality pitch used by the best Club sides in Southampton cricket and venue for the prestigious Sports Centre Knock-out Final. This jewel in Southampton's crown was created in the 1930s but these days the whole place has sadly declined. The little wooden 'pavilions' on each pitch have been removed after vandalism.

In 2015 ambitious plans for a £27 million revamp of the 150-acre site were revealed by the Council.

Ford Sports, Old Edwardians, Old Simmarians, Ordnance Survey, and Southern Gas are among the many Clubs to have used the Sports Centre for Hampshire League games.

SOUTHAMPTON – Wellington Sports Ground

Wellington Sports Ground was built in 1980 for Southampton University. Major refurbishment of the pavilion interior was taking place in 2016 when this photograph was taken.

The ground was transferred to Southampton's King Edward VI School in 2005 when the Wide Lane pitches were opened.

SOUTHWICK – Southwick House

This ground and pavilion is in the grounds of Southwick House, where the D-Day landings were planned.

The site became known as HMS *Dryad*, which was a shore establishment and the home of the Navy's Maritime Warfare School from the Second World War until they moved to HMS *Collingwood* in Fareham in 2004. It is now home to the Defence College of Policing and Guarding, who still play cricket here.

SOUTH WONSTON

This is the old pavilion that was there when South Wonston had a cricket team. It was demolished to make way for a new one which was opened on 18 September 2016 by Lawrie McMenemy MBE, the former Southampton Football Club manager. Sadly there is no provision for cricket here now.

STANSTED PARK HOUSE

Although in West Sussex, Stansted Park Cricket Club had seven years in the Hampshire League between 1975 and 1981.

A new Stansted Park Cricket Club was formed in 2008 when, they say - 'old friends realized that it made sense to merge Old Eldonians Cricket Club and Rowlands Castle Cricket Club to form a single stronger club and continue the tradition of this great game which has been played at Stansted Park, on the lawn in front of the stately home, since 1741 when Slindon played Portsmouth'.

STOCKTON – Recreation Ground

Stockton is a small village in the Wylye Valley. Cricket probably reached Wiltshire by the end of the 17th century but the earliest known reference is dated 1769.

Former Prime Minister John Major wrote 'that cricket did not spread evenly across whole counties but had a tendency towards local adoption'. He mentions a match at Stockton in 1799 which was reported as 'an event so novel in the county of Wiltshire', but cricket was by then being played at several other venues in the county.

Stockton Cricket Club joined the Hampshire League in 2002 but left in 2008.

STRATFIELD TURGIS – Turgis Green

Stratfield Turgis & Hartley Wespall Cricket Club's emblem, bearing 1811 as the founding date, 'lacks hard substantiation' they say.

They were members of the Hampshire League from 1973 to 1977. However, an Extraordinary General Meeting on 19 April 1977 decided that they join the Berkshire League, where they now play.

In 1972 Tylehurst St George Cricket Club had begun ground-sharing and they eventually decided to merge in 1981. The newly installed bar was opened on 25 May 1979. In 1989 the pavilion was 'vastly improved' and by 1994 the Berkshire League had pronounced the ground and clubhouse 'fit for Premier' status.

SULHAMSTEAD – Jack's Booth Ground – The Watson Oval

This pavilion was opened on 24 June 1990 by Peter May, the former captain of Surrey and England.

Berkshire's Sulhamstead & Ufton Cricket Club played in the Hampshire League from 1976 to 2007 and this was perhaps the most distant out-of-county club to have played in the League.

Known affectionately to many as 'Sully', they can trace their origins back to the 1880s. There are two squares here and the main pitch is another that has a large tree within the boundary.

TOTTON – British American Tobacco Company Ground

This pavilion was built in June 1964. The original clubhouse was built in 1927 in the corner of the ground adjacent to the railway line.

Formed in 1928 and known as Bramtoco Sports Cricket Club, the name changed to BAT Cricket Club around 1978. It changed again in 2007 to Totton & Eling Cricket Club following the closure of the British American Tobacco Company. The ground was re-vamped and a new pavilion built. See Part 1.

TWYFORD – Twyford School

The Jimmy Adams Pavilion. Named after and opened by Jimmy Adams of Hampshire County Cricket Club, at his alma mater, on 4 July 2015.

Twyford School moved to this site in 1809 and is said to be the oldest preparatory school in the United Kingdom.

UPHAM – The Holt

This is the pavilion that was replaced by the present one around 1975. The Club that played here then was the Preshaw and Holt Cricket Club. They were named after two country manor-houses. Preshaw House was built in the early 18th century, and The Holt, which is a Grade II listed building.

The current owners of this ground, which is in 'the middle of nowhere' only require it for one game a year, so are happy to have a resident club to look after it.

WARNFORD – Hampshire Hogs Ground

This pavilion was opened in 1974 by Cecil Paris, the former captain of Hampshire CCC who became President of the MCC after being nominated by Prince Philip, who he succeeded, in 1975.

The Hampshire Hogs Cricket Club was founded in 1887 when it was known as The Northland Rover Cricket Club. They play mainly declaration cricket against a variety of clubs that include the MCC, Free Foresters, and I Zingari. Almost all of the 50 or so annual fixtures are played here in the Meon Valley, which has been their home since 1966.

WEST HILL PARK SCHOOL

This pavilion was opened by John Crawley the Lancashire, Hampshire, and England batsman, on 9 July 2003. West Hill Park School near Titchfield was established in 1920 by Charles Ransome and lies in 28 acres of land, much of which is used for sport.

WEST MEON

A plaque on the wall says: 'In memory of Andrew James Morley, Chairman 1986-1994. To sportsmen who should pass this way enjoy your sport and see fair play. A.J.'

This is West Meon & Warnford Cricket Club's home. The club goes back a long way. In 1825 West Meon Cricket Club played a game against Medstead. The winner's trophy was a large bell which had been found in a barn near the cricket field. The story goes that Medstead won the match and trophy, which forms part of the church peal to this day. True or not, it's a good story. The match was played at West Meon, the ground at that time probably being at the end of Floud Lane.

Thomas Lord, founder of the world's most famous cricket ground, died in West Meon on 13 January 1832 and lies only 200 yards away from the ground in the graveyard of St John's Church.

WEST MOORS – Fryer Field

Fryer Field is a large recreation ground located to the north of this East Dorset village and has facilities for football, tennis, basketball and cricket.

West Moors Cricket Club played here between 2002 and 2012 before becoming Ferndown & Wayfarers Cricket Club in 2013, when they moved to Dolmans Farm.

WEST TYTHERLEY – Norman Court School

This pavilion is on the pitch in front of the manor house. The original pitch here is just outside the school grounds. It had an elegant pavilion that remains today as a private house.

The Norman Court School nestles amidst 45 acres of beautiful woodland and countryside, on the border of Hampshire and Wiltshire, in a Grade 2 listed manor house that was previously owned by Washington Merritt Singer, the son of the sewing machine magnate.

WEST TYTHERLEY – Norman Court School

This is the pavilion that is now a private house. It was the original pavilion on the original ground which has not been used since at least 1955 when the school first arrived here from its previous home in Kent.

WHERWELL – Playing Fields

The Andover Timber Company supplied and erected this pavilion for £615.19s.0d and the first event was held here on the 6 August 1956. It was demolished in 2011, eleven years after the new pavilion was built. See Part 1.

Wherwell Cricket Club was founded in 1868 and played at Priory Park but on 1 January 1888 Captain Victor Montagu, who owned the field, withdrew permission to use it so they moved to a new ground near Fullerton Station which cost them £7.7s.0d. In 1955 they had to vacate that ground too, and this field was donated by Anna Jenkins. Hilliers Nurseries laid the square and did the ground-work for the astonishingly low sum of £200.

WHITEPARISH – Memorial Ground

This pavilion was knocked down in 2013 and replaced by the one shown in Part 1.

WIELD – The Hook

Cricket here was introduced by Fred Messenger, landlord of the adjacent Yew Tree Inn until 1912.

There were pauses during the two world-wars, and in 1945 work started to recreate the ground, but in the early 1950s it came to an end. The Salter family came to the Yew Tree in 1979, and after a meeting on 27 August 1979, Wield Cricket Club was born again, using a portaloo and an old mobile home as a 'pavilion'. The present pavilion was opened in July 1988. The club is famous for its wonderful teas. A book has been published - Cricket and Teas, by Margaret Salter. The book is a compilation of recipes and sandwich ideas which have delighted players and supporters of Wield Cricket Club since 1981.

The fixture list shows a heavy bias, not unsurprisingly considering the above, towards Home games.

WINCHESTER COLLEGE – Kingsgate Park

Winchester College was founded in 1382. The game of Cricket came a little later, but today the College has seven cricket squares, on four grounds, and three pavilions.

This one is on the western side of the road from the other College grounds. Meads is the one nearest the city and is an enclosed ground. New Field has three squares – Lavender Meads, Lords, which is the main one, and Doggers. Then there is Gater Field which has Gater 1 and Gater 2.

Lavender Meads, Doggers and Gater Field do not have separate pavilions.

WINCHESTER COLLEGE – Lords, New Field

The Hunter Tent pavilion was built in 1930. The ground dates from 1869. Hunter Tent was dedicated to Richard Jocelyn Hunter and his brothers Hugh and Robert.

The plaque in the pavilion reads: This Tent, built in 1930, was given to the School in memory of ROBERT CECIL HUNTER Lords 1896-7, died Nov 1921 RICHARD JOCELYN HUNTER Lords 12th man 1905, killed in France Aug 1918 HUGH MICHAEL HUNTER Lords 1910, died of wounds in France April 1915, and replaces the Tent given in memory of HERBERT ROSS WEBBE Capt of Lords 1875.

This is the main College ground, and has hosted one first-class match when on 19-20 August 1875 Kent beat Hampshire by an innings and 217 runs.

WINCHESTER COLLEGE – Meads

The Frazer Tent pavilion was opened in 1930. This stone and flint pavilion was built in memory of JE Frazer, a boy who was a pupil at the College between 1914 and 1920 and who died in January 1927.

The Latin inscription along the eaves of the delightful pavilion says: CVI DOMVS HIS CAMPIS FVERAT DILECTIOR VLLA HANC POSVIT PVERIS ET PVER IPSE DOMVM.

The College Head of Classics translated it thus: He for whom a house on these fields had been more loved than any put this house (here) for the boys and was himself a boy.

WINCHESTER – Garrison Ground

The pavilion here is in poor condition and the ground has not been used for cricket for many years.

Tesco owned this site at Bar End and planned to build on it, but it was bought by Winchester Council in November 2016. The Council have plans to replace the North Walls Leisure Centre with a brand-new £34 million one here, and so preserve the site for sport.

WINTERSLOW

This is the pavilion at Winterslow Cricket Club's previous ground, which they vacated in 2009 when they moved to Barry's Field. See Part 1.

YATELEY – The Tythings, Yateley Green

This is the pavilion at Yateley Cricket Club's previous ground, before they moved to the Sean Devereux Park in 1999. See Part 1.

There has been a high degree of change on Yateley Green over the years, with the former manager's house being converted into offices for the Town Council. A purpose-built premises was provided for the Council in 1981. An adjoining sports pavilion was first approved in 1969 but was demolished in the 1990s when The Tythings was built.

✿ PART 3 ✿

Isle of Wight Grounds

This part includes Ventnor Cricket Club who play in the Southern Premier League at Newclose and in the Hampshire League at their traditional home at Steephill. It also includes Ryde, Ryde Cavaliers, and Shanklin Cricket Clubs, who all played in the Hampshire League in 2016, and Brading Cricket Club who are past members.

The Isle of Wight is the largest island in England and was part of Hampshire until 1890. It became the 39th official county in English cricket and the Isle of Wight Cricket Board organise an internal cricket league between various local clubs. In November 2010 the Isle of Wight Cricket Board discussed with the Minor Counties Cricket Association and the England and Wales Cricket Board, proposals to enter a side in the Minor Counties tournaments.

Many of the grounds and clubs will be familiar to those on the Mainland since the Island is a favourite for touring teams. Newclose hosted Hampshire Second XI for a three-day game against Kent at the end of July 2016 and so joined JS White's in Cowes, Shanklin, and the nearby Victoria Ground in Newport as grounds that have hosted the County Club in competitive matches. Some of the other grounds will be less well known and there will be others at schools and those without pavilions, that aren't included.

The Isle of Wight Cricket Board lists 45 clubs in 2016, so the 21 grounds featured in this section may not tell the complete story.

In 2016 the Island Saturday League was sponsored by Leslies Motors.

ARRETON – Heasley Lane

ARRETON CC and BINSTEAD CC: The pavilion is a converted holiday-camp gymnasium which became available in 1976. Arreton had a claim to fame in the English calendar. It was the venue for what was for many years listed in the Cricketer magazine as the last properly scheduled match of the English season. For more than twenty years on the final Sunday in October they hosted The Mallishags, an old Island word for a caterpillar which is particularly slow in the field. The day before, Arreton's neighbours Havenstreet played the Rest of the Whirled. The two matches were devised, arranged, managed and publicised by Mac Richards, an eccentric owner of a second-hand bookshop in Newport. Arreton Cricket Club was founded in 1968 and they play in the Leslies Motors League. Binstead Cricket Club share the ground with Arreton, and they only play midweek Friendlies.

BEMBRIDGE – Steyne Park

BEMBRIDGE CC: This building houses the changing rooms, but tea is usually taken in the building next to it.

The ground is owned and operated by Bembridge Parish Council and is used for football and petanque as well as cricket, and is the home of the Bembridge Youth and Community Centre.

A fun cricket match was held on 24 April 2016 against Wootton to officially open the new all-weather wicket and general improvements at the ground. The full project cost £13,463 which was raised from grants and donations. Bembridge Cricket Club play in the Leslies Motors League.

BRADING – Middlemead

BRADING CC: Middlemead was purchased in 1987. The first match was against Wimbledon United Cricket Club on 1 July 1989. The pavilion was officially opened on 5 July 1992 with a game against Jim Parks' Old England XI.

There is a painting in the Lords pavilion of a cricket match at Brading in 1750. The present Brading Cricket Club was formed as the Wheatsheaf Taverners Cricket Club in 1976 and played at Havenstreet.

In 1977 they re-named themselves Brading Cricket Club and moved to a ground at the South Wight Sports Centre in Sandown. Brading played in the Hampshire League between 2002 and 2007, but now only play Friendlies against touring parties and local sides.

With four pubs in this small town near the coast, it's a favourite destination for touring cricket clubs.

BRIGHSTONE – New Road

BRIGHSTONE CC: This ground and pavilion date from the late 1960s and the pavilion was refurbished in 2013.

Brighstone Cricket Club had a fixture list comprising mostly of touring sides on Saturdays and Sundays. Unfortunately, after existing for 120 years, the Club folded at the end of 2015 due to lack of players.

The village lies within an Area of Outstanding Beauty, and its coastline is designated as a Heritage Coast and Site of Special Scientific Interest.

COWES – J Samuel White's Ground

COWES CC: Shipbuilders J Samuel White constructed the ground in 1953. It was opened by Mrs JA Milne on the 25 April 1953, followed by a match against a Hampshire XI. A photograph in the pavilion shows that it was a full-strength Hampshire side, captained by Desmond Eagar.

Hampshire played the first of seven first-class games at this ground with a drawn match against Worcestershire on 26 May 1956.

The ground was taken over by the Plessey Company in the mid-1960s following the decline in ship-building and then became the Isle of Wight Community Club in 1984. It is now known as the Milne Memorial Ground.

Cowes Cricket Club play in the Leslies Motors League.

COWES – Northwood

NORTHWOOD CC: Northwood Cricket Club was formed in 1842. They occupy the land at Northwood Recreation Ground as a result of a gift by William George Ward in 1875.

This pavilion, which replaced two old army huts, was opened by Wilfred Ward, William's great-great grandson, on 15 September 1972. The £10,000 cost was met with help from a Lords Taverners donation, and a £5,500 loan from Cowes Council. The 150th anniversary of the Club in 1992 was celebrated with a match against the MCC. Northwood Cricket Club play in the Leslies Motors League.

EAST COWES – Osborne House

This former cricket pavilion was built for the cadets in the early 1900s when the Royal Naval College was established within the grounds of Osborne House. The College vacated the site in 1921 and the cricket ground was seldom used since then.

Today, Osborne House is under the care of English Heritage and is open to the public. The cricket pavilion was converted into a holiday cottage in 2004. Pavilion Cottage sleeps four and is available for rent year-round. Doors from the lounge and two bedrooms lead out onto the south facing veranda and onto the 'outfield'.

EAST COWES – Whippingham

EAST COWES CC: This ground and pavilion opened in 1994. East Cowes Cricket Club was re-formed in the 1950s and became the British Hovercraft Corporation CC when Saunders-Roe and Vickers-Supermarine merged in 1966. BHC became Westland Aerospace in 1984, and then GKN Aerospace in 1994, before the Club reverted to the East Cowes CC name again.

The original Club first played at a ground in Victoria Road and then another ground at Old Road which later became a housing estate, before moving here.

NEWPORT – Newclose

The ground was officially opened on 27 July 2009 by Mike Gatting. It is the Island's newest cricket ground which was created by the late Brian Gardener. Ventnor Cricket Club play their Southern Premier League games here. It is also the headquarters of the Isle of Wight Cricket Board (IWCB).

It is likely that the first ball was bowled here in a makeshift game on 6 September 2008, but a Newclose XI played Jim Parks' Old England XI on Sunday 7 June 2009.

Newclose Cricket Club was established in 2013 and play Friendlies on Sundays and are particularly keen to host touring teams visiting the Island. In September 2016 the ground was offered for sale for £1 million.

NEWPORT – Seaclose Recreation Ground

Seaclose Recreation Ground is better known as the site of the Isle of Wight Festival since 2002 when the Festival was revived.

The pavilion is still used by footballers when the musicians have gone, but the ground is not now used for cricket.

Medina Cricket Club used this ground, but have now disbanded.

NEWPORT – Victoria Recreation Ground

NEWPORT CC: This ground and pavilion opened in 1902. It is now known as Newport Victoria Sports & Social Club which was formed in 1983 by the amalgamation of the Newport Cricket, IW Hockey, Newport Victoria Sports, and the IW Ladies Hockey Clubs.

Medina Borough Council gave them £17,500 to upgrade the facilities and they also got £2,000 from the National Sports Council. In 2014 there were fears it would close because the £4,000 annual Council-grant was to be axed. It meant the pavilion might be pulled down and the recreation ground closed. However, the ground's future was secured when Newport Parish Council agreed to take over the lease and pledged £7,600 to the upkeep of the pavilion. Newport Cricket Club play in the Leslies Motors League.

NEWPORT – Whitecroft, Sandy Lane

WHITECROFT CC: The ground doubles-up as a football pitch, with an astroturf wicket for cricket.

The ground is located next door to the former Whitecroft Hospital which opened in 1896 as the Isle of Wight County Asylum and closed in 1992, and is said to be haunted.

Whitecroft Cricket Club play in the Leslies Motors League.

NITON – Allotment Road

NITON CC: Niton Cricket Club have disbanded since this photograph was taken in 2006. This ground, on a very steep slope, is not used for cricket any more.

PORCHFIELD – Colemans Lane

PORCHFIELD CC and ISLAND BAKERIES CC: The Porchfield Cricket and Community Club pavilion here was opened on 27 June 1987 by Jack Rogers, President of Ventnor Cricket Club. The oldest record of a game involving Porchfield Cricket Club was a match between the 'Singles' and 'Marrieds' on 25 July 1893. The ground then was a field behind the Homestead in Main Road. Around 1912 they moved to Locks Farm before moving again in 1919 to Brooks Glen in New Road where they stayed until the move to Colemans Lane in 1987. The ground was bought for £8,000 and the pavilion cost a further £11,500 in materials, but was built by Club members. It was extended in 2006. Island Bakeries Cricket Club was formed in 1975 as a works side playing evening 20-over matches. The Bakery in Binstead closed in 1984 but it was decided to keep the cricket club going and retain the name. They started playing at Pell Lane in Ryde before moving to Simeon Street, Ryde in 1992, and then to Porchfield in 1996. Both sides play Friendlies against touring sides and other Isle of Wight teams.

ROOKLEY – Community Centre

GODSHILL CC: Godshill Cricket Club was formed in the early 1950s by Don Charles and played at Sandford, a small hamlet to the east of Godshill. They then played in the village at Rongsfield until around 2007 when they moved to nearby Rookley.

This community centre at Rookley opened in 2001 following extensive fund raising and grants from Sport for All and the Lottery Fund. The ground only has an astroturf wicket so Godshill Cricket Club used Newclose for their Saturday games in the Leslies Motors League in 2016, and the Rookley ground on Sundays for their Friendly matches.

RYDE – Harding Shute

RYDE CC: Ryde Cricket Club dates back to 1829 and has had several home grounds. Between 1829 and 1878 they played at Quarr Hill and Ryde House. From 1879 to 1939 it was Partlands. The Club re-formed after the war and between 1948 and 1950 they used St John's House before moving to Smallbrook Heath until 1962. They next went to Simeon Street Recreation Ground before making Harding Shute their permanent home. The first game played here was an inter-Club challenge in June 1989.

CB Fry (1902) and Jack Hobbs (1939) both played against Ryde, and Australian Test captain Alan Border guested for them in 1986 against the Old England XI.

Ryde First XI play in the Southern League, with their Second XI in the Hampshire League.

RYDE – Smallbrook Stadium

RYDE CAVALIERS CC: Ryde Cavaliers Cricket Club was founded in 1971 and played at a ground in Ashey. They moved to Smallbrook in the early 1980s before the Stadium was there. The Ryde Speedway team was founded in 1995 and the Cricket Club use their facilities for changing and entertaining.

Ryde Cavaliers played in the Island Saturday League until they joined the Hampshire League in 2016.

SHANKLIN – Westhill

SHANKLIN CC: The present pavilion was formally opened in 1964. A photograph of a dinner held in the pavilion is captioned thus: To commemorate the official opening of the new club pavilion by our patron, the late Admiral of the Fleet Earl Mountbatten of Burma, KG, PC, GCB, OM, GCSI, GCIE, GCVO, DSO, ADC. (July 19th 1964) LORD'S TAVERNERS v SHANKLIN CC.

It is said that Shanklin Cricket Club's roots go back to 1871. Wally Hammond captained Shanklin when they played Ventnor on 5 May 1951 in a match to celebrate the re-opening of the ground after the war.

Shanklin First XI play in the Hampshire League and their Second XI in the Leslies Motors League. They also have a Sunday team, a Midweek team, and the over-40 'Evergreens' team who play on Thursdays.

ST HELENS – The Green

ST HELENS CC: St Helens is a village that was built around village greens, and The Green, also known as Goose Island, is where the cricket team play. The St Helens Sports Association was formed in 2004 with the intent of building a new pavilion for the use of the local Blue Star Football Club, Cricket Club, and Petanque players. With funding from the Football Foundation, Biffaward, local businesses, and residents, this pavilion was built in 2008.

Nearby is St Helens Duver, a sand-dune complex where the first golf course on the island was located. The Duver is no longer a golf course and is maintained by the National Trust.

St Helens Cricket Club play in the Leslies Motors League.

VENTNOR – Steephill

VENTNOR CC: The Ventnor Academy cost £1.5 million and was opened on 25 July 2003 by Lord MacLaurin, the ECB Chairman. It replaced the pavilion that cost £2,600 which opened on 29 April 1973 at this unique 'ground in a bowl' next to the Botanic Garden. Ventnor Cricket Club celebrated its 150th Anniversary in 2000, although there is evidence of a Club before 1850. Formed initially as the Undercliffe Cricket Club they played at various sites around Ventnor until they established a permanent home at Steephill where the first game was on 20 August 1885. The first pavilion opened on 1 August 1892. In 1897 Ventnor Cricket Club was born after financial problems ended the days of the Undercliffe Club. Jack Hobbs played for Ventnor against Sandown on 27 June 1931.

This ground was deemed unsuitable for Premier League cricket because of its steep slopes, so the Ventnor First XI now play at Newclose. Their Second and Third XIs play in the Hampshire League.

WOOTTON – Recreation Ground

WOOTTON CC: And finally, this brick pavilion on the Recreation Ground is used by the Isle of Wight Rugby Football Club, and was officially opened on 19 September 1971. It was extended in 1975. The cricketers and their guests have to change in the converted containers next to it. The wicket is an artificial one.

The first hut on the Recreation Ground was completed in 1950 after farmer AE Long agreed to sell the land to the Council in 1946. The charge for using the hut was 3s.6d.

Wootton Cricket Club have one men's team and one women's team, both playing Friendly cricket only.

About the author

The youngest of four brothers, the author was introduced to cricket at a very young age. Returning from our evacuation home, the Chewton Glen at New Milton, in 1946, the family moved into an old house in Cobden Avenue, Bitterne Park, Southampton. Tony, the eldest brother, quickly modified the tennis court for use as a five-a-side football pitch and a cricket 'net'. In 1950 we moved to a brand-new house, 54 Woodmill Lane, only about 500 yards from the bungalow which the family had hurriedly left in 1939 (the bungalow was bombed days later). The side-way at 54 was soon our 'net' and one of my first 'coaches' was Nat Gonella, the jazz singer/trumpeter, who lived nearby. He tried to teach me the art of leg-spin, but I just wanted to bowl fast! By 1953 I was in the school team, playing on a coconut-matting-covered concrete strip at Bitterne Park Recreation Ground. The following appeared in the Silver Jubilee Magazine published by Bitterne Park School in 1964:

> 1955 began with Elliott taking 6 wickets for 8 runs followed by 8 wickets for 6 runs in matches won. An oddity in the match v. Ascupart was that B.P.'s Davis was out to Davis of Ascupart and he in turn was out to Davis of B.P. In the meantime, Davis had been taking wickets in matches - 1 for 6 runs, 2 for 4, 4 for 12, 6 wickets for 12. Then came the sensation. In a match against Northam "Todge" Davis was unplayable. In six overs, 5 of which were maidens, he took all ten wickets for 1 run - 5 wickets falling to him in one over and all bowled! This was followed by 4 wickets for 5, 5 for 20 and then 7 wickets for 1 run. In this very successful season his haul was 46 wickets for 90 runs. In the meantime Elliott was generally taking wickets at the other end - 37 in all. In view of these bowling achievements there was little need for batting displays though Elliott scored 19 and John Coles had 20 not out and 19 not out.

Tony Davis's performance against Northam was remarkable. I haven't seen 5 wickets in an over, or 10 in an innings, since.

Other than the side-way, our 'grass' pitch was Dolly's Field, a small patch of bomb-cratered land located below Dell Road, where the new Bitterne Park School now stands. Northlands Road was only a penny bus-ride away and I started going there in 1951 and joined Hampshire as a full member in 1965. My first Test Match experience was England versus Pakistan at the Oval in 1954.

Following five years at Taunton's School, where my only cricket was as Captain of the house team, a career as a draughtsman started at the Hampshire Aeroplane Club at Eastleigh, but I left and joined a contract drawing office in Southampton which indirectly led to me playing in the Parks Leagues. In 1963 I was assigned to IBM at Hursley where I was welcomed into the Cricket Club. After 9 years as a sub-contractor and a regular in the cricket and football teams, IBM employed me. A career-change followed after attending Art College and the rest of my working life was as an Illustrator in the Publications department. Flying, my other life-long love, resulted in a PPL in 1992, but it all came to an end in 1996 when I got sick, but that is another story.